The Catholicism of
Shakespeare's Plays

The Catholicism of Shakespeare's Plays

by

Peter Milward SJ

The Saint Austin Press
1997

THE SAINT AUSTIN PRESS
PO Box 610
Southampton
SO14 0YY

© 1997, Peter Milward SJ

ISBN 1 901157 10 5

Front cover: Anne Hathaway's Cottage, Stratford.
© Peter Milward

Contents

Preface

There is a strange enigma hanging over the plays and personality of England's greatest poet and dramatist. Was the dramatist really William Shakespeare of Stratford-upon-Avon, as most people assume? Or was he someone else, according to one or other theory of authorship? And in any case, what kind of a man was he who wrote such plays and poems of genius? And what was his attitude to the many problems facing the Englishmen of his time, not the least of which was the religious problem.

All the same, little as we know about the dramatist himself, there is no lack of biographies about him. These, however, consist largely of background information; but as they approach his personality, they become increasingly vague and conjectural. Assuming the identity of the dramatist to be William Shakespeare of Stratford-upon-Avon, we have few more facts about him than those of his birth, marriage and death, together with the similar facts about his parents and children. There are also a few legal documents relating to him, in which his name is mentioned. Otherwise, we only have his writings, the plays and the poems; and of these, the plays are strangely impersonal, while the poems, for all their personality, leave us all the more baffled about their biographical relevance.

Even when we turn to the historical background, under the last of the Tudors, Elizabeth I (1558-1603), and the first of the Stuarts, James I (1603-1625), we find the situation strangely murky in the matter of most importance, the religious problem. This problem goes back to the decision of Henry VIII to reject the authority of Rome concerning the matter of his divorce, and so effectively to establish a new Church of England with himself as its head. He went on to dissolve all the monasteries of his kingdom, over 600 of them, partly to enrich himself, partly to buy the support of the gentry for the religious changes he was setting afoot. Then, after a period of fluctuation between the Protestant policy of his son Edward VI and the Catholic policy of his daughter Mary, it was under his other daughter Elizabeth that the Church of England was finally established – as Protestant in all places of authority, but Catholic in sympathy among large sections of the lesser clergy and the people. In the course of her reign, moreover, there also appears a contrast between the more radical of the Protestants known as "Puritans" and the more heroic of the Catholics who were ready to suffer for their religion and were known as "Recusants" for their refusal to attend the new English services.

All this is clear enough in such general terms. But now the question arises as to how Shakespeare fits into this pattern of religion in Elizabethan England. How far did he go along with all these religious changes? Or to what extent did he disagree with them – whether as a Puritan, considering that they failed to go far enough, or as a Recusant, or at least a Church-Papist (as secret Catholic sympathisers were called), lamenting the changes? From the little that is known of his biography, it is hard to tell; but from what we know of both his parents, there are certain indications that they both had to suffer for the old faith. In the 1580s the family of his mother, Mary Arden, had to endure the inquisition of the local Puritan magistrate, Sir Thomas Lucy, concerning the Somerville plot to kill the Queen (as Somerville was connected by marriage with the Ardens). About the same time we find Shakespeare's father John increasingly troubled by financial and legal difficulties, till he appears on a list of recusants in 1592 while pleading fear "of process for debt". Such facts may well be interpreted in a Catholic sense, while falling short of certainty; but even so, they tell us little about the allegiance of the dramatist himself, at least in his subsequent career on the stage.

Anyhow, leaving aside the vexed questions of biography, what, it may be asked, may be learnt from the plays? They are charged with topical references, enabling editors to decide on the propable dates of their composition and/or first performance. Only, it seems, the dramatist for the most part avoids mention of the religious controversies that were still occupying the minds of his contemporaries, whether between Catholic and Protestant, or between Anglican and Puritan. This avoidance may well have been because such mention was too dangerous, seeing how closely connected were religion and politics in that age – especially if there was any sign of sympathy with the old faith, which the Elizabethan government under Lord Burghley was bent on supressing.

There are indeed a few references to these controversies that have been detected in the plays, but they are mostly of a non-committal nature. Thus Mercutio's exclamation on being mortally pierced by Tybalt's rapier in *Romeo and Juliet* (iii.1), "A plague o' both your houses!"; Helena's lament in *A Midsummer Night's Dream* (iii.2) at the way "truth kills truth, O devilish-holy fray!"; Hamlet's criticism of his mother for having committed "such a deed as ... sweet religion makes a rhapsody of words" (iii.4); Lucio's remark in *Measure for Measure* (i.2), "Grace is grace, despite of all controversy" – in so far as they may well be applied to the religious controversies of the time, seem to imply a distaste for such controversy on the part of the dramatist, coupled with a high regard for "sweet religion". Still, it need not mean that Shakespeare was adopting an attitude of sitting on the fence, avoiding any commitment to either side. All it means is that he was unable, from the nature of his situation, to express his commitment in an open manner.

In approaching particular plays, however, we have to be careful not to think in terms of the twentieth century, in which religion is free, but of the sixteenth century, when there was no such freedom in Elizabethan England. In the time of Shakespeare, all Englishmen were bound by law to be Anglican, to attend the new English service according to the Book of Common Prayer, and to recognise the Queen, not the Pope, as supreme governor of the Church in England – or else suffer the severe penalties determined by law. Thus the Elizabethan Church, so far from being a *via media* of wise toleration between the fanatical extremes of Popery and Puritanism, was a persecuting Church as well against the Papists as against the Puritans – and perhaps chiefly against the former, as the latter at least accepted the Queen as supreme governor of the Church.

Hence if Shakespeare was other than a conforming member of the Anglican Church, and especially if he sympathized with the Catholic recusants, he was obliged to keep his religious opinions to himself; or if he expressed them, it could only be done in disguise, at a remove from his real meaning. In this meaning he might well have exclaimed, in the words of Hamlet, "But break, my heart, for I must hold my tongue!" (i.2). In this meaning he might well have identified himself with the fantastical Duke in *Measure for Measure*, of whom Lucio remarks that "His givings out were of an infinite distance/ From his true-meant design" (i.4). In this meaning his speeches may well have been designed to hit the thoughts of sympathizers in his audience who could, as Lennox tells another Lord in *Macbeth* (iii.6), "interpret further."

No doubt, there were Puritan recusants, who refused to conform to the established Church. They were the Brownists, followers of Robert Browne, and other separatists, who were eventually driven into exile for their non-conformity in the Low Countries; and eventually some of them made their way to New England. But in his plays Shakespeare has little to say in their favour: rather "Puritan" is mostly a word of ridicule in them, though he is less of a Puritan-baiter than his friend and colleague, Ben Jonson (who was for a time an open recusant, in the Catholic sense). As for the Brownists, we have the well-known asseveration of Sir Andrew Aguecheek in *Twelfth Night* (iii.2), "I had as lief be a Brownist as a politician" – in which one may discern the dramatist's own feelings with regard both to Brownists and to politicians. On the other hand, in contrast to the frequent mention of Puritans, there are in the plays only two references to Papists: one in the related form of "Popish", where it is put into the mouth of the villain Aaron the Moor in *Titus Andronicus* (v.l), with implicit praise of Lucius' "religious conscience"; and the other in *All's Well That Ends Well* (i.3), where the Clown's mention of "old Poysam the papist" is immediately criticized by the Countess as "foul-mouthed and calumnious". At least, in this contrast we may suspect the direction in which the dramatist's sympathies lie.

With all this in mind, we may now turn to a representative number of plays for more precise examination, in view not so much of occasional expressions that may be interpreted in one way or another, as of their prevailing tendency – if at a level beneath what is obvious to any audience. In this sense, the plays may not unfairly be regarded as parables, as George Herbert says in "Jordan", "Catching the sense at two removes", or as the clown Launce tells his counterpart in *Two Gentlemen of Verona* (ii.4), "Thou shalt never get such a secret from me but by a parable."

The Merchant of Venice

Partly for its happy ending in marriage, partly for the comic scenes featuring Launcelot Gobbo and his old father, *The Merchant of Venice* is customarily classed among the comedies of Shakespeare. Yet it is remarkably serious in content and comes as close to tragedy as any of the comedies. In its content we are specially impressed by the Biblical contrast between the Jews, represented by Shylock, and the Christians, represented by most of the other characters, particularly Antonio and Portia. This is also a contrast between the legal justice of the Old Law and the ideal mercy of the New Law. It thus marks a further development in Shakespeare's dramaturgy, as the first of the "mature comedies", with emphasis on the Biblical theme of "mercy" that is again taken up in the problem comedy of *Measure for Measure*.

Considering this notably religious content of the play, we may well ask to what extent it may be seen as reflecting the religious controversies of Elizabethan England. To be sure, the scene is set in Renaissance Venice, where the Christians are all Catholic: they could hardly be anything else. The only non-Catholics are the Jews: Shylock himself, his friend Tubal, and his daughter Jessica up till her elopement with the Christian Lorenzo. On the other hand, Shakespeare had presumably never visited the city of Venice; and so he could only depict it in terms that were more familiar to him, namely the city of London. After all, however far he may roam in his plays to distant ages and places, he is ever thinking of his own age and place, according to the principle, "There's no place like home." For him, as for Hamlet, players are "the abstracts and brief chronicles of the time", and the plays they enact are means by which he seeks to "catch the conscience" of the people.

To begin with the most impressive character, Shylock, he is introduced to us – it should be emphasized – not so much as a Jew of the Old Testament, but rather as a moneylender, one of the few employments open to Jews in Christian countries. Then in so far as Venice is London, Shylock might well have been recognized by an Elizabethan audience in terms not so much of the Jews, who were still banned from entry into England, as of the Puritan merchants of London. For one thing, these merchants not infrequently lent money at usurious rates of interest. For another, they were called "Christian Jews" for their familiarity with the Old Testament and their habit of christening their children with names derived from Old Testament personages, rather than with names of Christian saints. For yet another, they were strict and sober, insisting on hard work, according to what came to be known as "the Puritan work-ethic", while despising others as "sons of Belial". And so they kept apart from others, refusing not only to worship with them but also to eat or drink with them. In all these and other matters Shylock appears in this play exactly as the Puritans are described in contemporary records.

Nowadays, with the modern rejection of anything savouring of racial or religious discrimination, it is common for people – whether producers or spectators, whether scholars or students – to sympathize with Shylock and to see him as an unfortunate object of discrimination, till he comes to seem rather the hero than the villain, and he rather than Antonio is identified with the "merchant" of the title. Attention is paid to Antonio's abuse of him as "cutthroat dog", while spitting on his "Jewish gaberdine". Further emphasis is laid on his pitiful speech beginning, "Hath not a Jew eyes?", and culminating, "If you wrong us, shall we not revenge?" All this seems to justify his refusal to have any mercy on Antonio, and even to make Portia's appeal for mercy sound hypocritical. Indeed, not a few members of the audience today are hardly to be satisfied short of the shedding of Antonio's blood! All this, however, overlooks the emphasis and the tendency of the play itself, in view of the age in which it was written and first performed. Shylock is, after all, as I have pointed out, not so much Jewish as Puritan in his characterization, with emphasis on the fact that he is a moneylender. If he is criticized by Antonio and his friends, for his "cutthroat" practices, it is not so much because he is a Jew as because he is a moneylender, lending money to people in need at exorbitant rates of interest. Thus the play is not so much anti-Semitic, against the Jews as such, as anti-Puritan, in so far as the Puritan merchants went in for money-lending – and also, it may be remembered, for opposition to plays. In the play, moreover, Shylock is shown not as discriminated against for being a Jew (except in his own, self-pitying words), but as hating the Christians and as having the power, put into his hands by the laws of Venice, to satisfy his hatred. Up till almost the last moment in the trial scene it seems as if even one Jew, so long as he has the law on his side, can have his own way – amounting to judicial murder – against all the assembled Christians.

Now what about the other characters, who are mostly Christian, that is to say, in contemporary Venetian terms Catholic? How are they to be interpreted in corresponding terms of Shakespeare's London, where most of the Christians would have been conforming Anglicans?

To begin with the merchant himself, Antonio, once the period of his loan has expired, becomes the prisoner of Shylock with the certainty of death awaiting him. His reason for seeking the loan and for his subsequent arrest on being unable to repay the loan is his friendship with Bassanio, whom he thus enables to go abroad and win the hand of the lady Portia. From the outset, at the beginning of the play, there is an aura of mystery surrounding him even in his own eyes, "In sooth, I know not why I am so sad." He is, like the dramatist himself, an enigma. In the tragic outcome, when he is shown in Shylock's power, he is described as "one in whom the ancient Roman honour more appears" than in anyone else.

Now, putting all these points together, in Antonio, as contrasted with Shylock, we may well find them most applicable in terms of Shakespeare's London not just to the Catholic Recusants, but more precisely to the priests and especially the Jesuits as being the chief object of Puritan hatred and hostility. This hostility was shown not least in the House of Commons, where the number of Puritans was out of all proportion to their number in the country, and where it was they who mainly promoted the penal laws against Catholic Recusants, especially priests and Jesuits. As for these priests, it was a particular concern of theirs to send promising young men abroad for their Catholic

16

education, many of whom returned to England as ordained priests. Thus the voyage of Bassanio may be interpreted as an allegorical pilgrimage, with the lady Portia standing for theological Wisdom and/or evangelical Poverty. Also as a "merchant", Antonio may be compared to not a few of these priests, who referred to themselves in cipher (to avoid detection in letters that were often intercepted) as "merchant", even with specific mention of Italian cities such as Venice. For they were indeed merchants, like the one in Christ's parable, in search of the "pearl of great price" for which they were prepared to sacrifice everything (Matt. 13:46).

As for Bassanio, on reaching Belmont, the home of the lady Portia, he at once proceeds to his trial in terms of a choice among three caskets. Before making his choice, however, he engages in a strangely riddling conversation with Portia. First, mention is made of "these naughty times", with an echo of an all too frequent theme in Shakespeare's plays and poems, combining criticism of the Elizabethan present and nostalgia for the mediaeval past. What is naughty about these times is, Portia implies, not only the putting of bars "between the owners and their rights" but also the increasing recourse to the torture of "the rack" on those arrested for "treason" for the purpose of enforcing a "confession". Such a torture was not so much mediaeval as precisely Elizabethan, and it was chiefly used on Catholic priests after their arrest and imprisonment in the Tower of London, not as a punishment but as a means of extracting information concerning the whereabouts of other priests and Catholics and consequently the whole network of the Catholic resistance to the Elizabethan "reformation". When, for instance, it was originally used on Edmund Campion and his fellows from 1581 onwards, it occasioned an outcry in the Catholic courts of Europe, necessitating an official answer from the pen of Lord Burghley himself.

When, therefore, Bassanio proceeds to make his choice, he reflects on the danger of trusting to merely "outward shows", as in the caskets of gold and silver, and he specially refers to "the seeming truth which cunning times put on to entrap the wisest". Such was the propaganda never before employed so systematically as by Lord Burghley, with intent to cast discredit on the priests returning to England, from the time of the arrival of Edmund Campion in England in 1580. Indeed, the number of pamphlets put out with this purpose, many of them directly traceable to Burghley himself, is altogether amazing. I have counted some 50 such printed pamphlets in the 1580's alone, most of them connected with Campion in person. Consequently, when Bassanio goes on to choose the leaden casket, this may not unreasonably be interpreted as denoting the Catholic cause in Elizabethan England, promising him nothing but (in Churchillian terms) "blood, toil, tears and sweat". Then, when he returns to Venice to help his friend Antonio, while Portia goes disguised as a lawyer, one may well be reminded of the way priests could only return to England in disguise.

Turning at last to the lady Portia, she is represented from the outset as living overseas in her beautiful mountain home of Belmont. The name itself is interesting, as being also the home of Campion's close friend, who later became a Jesuit brother in prison, Thomas Pounde of Belmont in

Hampshire. He was, moreover, cousin to Shakespeare's patron, the young Earl of Southampton. Portia's home is further associated with monasteries, still flourishing as in old mediaeval times, and with wayside crosses, typical signs of Catholic devotion. At the former Portia vows "to live in prayer and contemplation" all the time Bassanio is in Venice; and at the latter she is said, in company with her maid Nerissa, to be kneeling and praying "for happy wedlock hours".

Above all, when she comes to the trial scene disguised as a lawyer, she makes her celebrated appeal for mercy in a speech remarkably charged with Biblical echoes, making this the most religious of Shakespeare's plays to date. (Till then, his plays had been predominantly secular in keeping with an age still governed by an early proclamation against the use of plays for religious propaganda.) Here, it may be said, is the most impressive part of the play, when all action ceases while Portia is speaking; and through her mouth, it may be added, the dramatist himself addresses his audience with an impassioned plea for mercy to be exercised in real life beyond the limits of the theatre.

In that case, it may be asked, what was the point of such a plea for mercy in Shakespeare's London? Well, in view of all that has been said so far, here were the Puritans as chief persecutors of the Catholics, especially the priests, bringing them before courts of law and arraigning them according to laws passed by Parliament at their persuasion, with the full support of official propaganda. The parallel between Shylock v. Antonio and Puritan v. Catholic is surely obvious in such contemporary circumstances. And so the plea for mercy, which the dramatist puts into the mouth of Portia, must have been not only to the people, who could do nothing, but to those in positions of authority from the Queen downwards on behalf of Catholic priests whose only crime was to bring spiritual assistance to the suffering Catholics and a realization of their solidarity with the Church overseas. Such a plea we find already proposed by the Jesuit martyr Robert Southwell in his moving *Humble Supplication to Her Majesty*, though it was not printed till 1600, five years after his death; while an earlier plea was presented also to the Queen by the Jesuit companion of Campion, Robert Persons, in his *Brief Discourse* of 1580.

Not that I maintain the certainty of all this evidence. Rather, many are certain to remain unconvinced and to call for more demonstrative proof. What I am calling for, on the other hand, is an open mind to consider at least the strong possibility – in view of the mediaeval and Renaissance cast of mind, together with the circumstances of the Elizabethan age – that *The Merchant of Venice* has a contemporary application or relevance, as what may be called a "topical allegory", with a deeper level of meaning than that of the mere story. Granted this possibility, it is surprising how everything seems to fall into place – as G.K. Chesterton says of the Catholic claims in his *Orthodoxy* – with an almost uncanny accuracy. At least one may say that Catholic members of the original audiences of the play, while enjoying the performance as a dramatized story, may well have noticed a deeper level of relevance to themselves to which Protestant members would have been largely oblivious. Or if the latter had suspected it and accused the dramatist of recusant sympathies, Shakespeare might well have challenged them to prove it – just as unfriendly critics may challenge me to prove it! After all, it would have been dangerous for the dramatist to have made his meaning any clearer, since then he might have been arrested or at least prevented by the Elizabethan censorship from any further utterance. Nor is it only in this one play that such a "topical allegory" may be discerned; but almost all his plays, especially those from *The Merchant* onwards, are subject in different ways to the same interpretation.

As You Like It

The Merchant of Venice is by no means the only play of Shakespeare's in which such a topical meaning, with reference to the situation of Elizabethan Catholics, may be discerned. If it was the only such play, the presence of such a meaning might well be suspected. But almost all the plays, I venture to say, may be seen to bear this topical allegory in an accumulation of evidence, all pointing in a variety of ways to one end and so amounting to what Newman in his *Grammar of Assent* terms "a convergence of probabilities".

To begin with, while *The Merchant* may be regarded as the first of the mature comedies for its serious, Biblical theme, yet even into the earliest and lightest of Shakespeare's comedies it is noteworthy how serious, even tragic elements insist on entering. In *The Comedy of Errors*, for instance, the amusing episodes arise for the most part from the accident of two pairs of identical twins (wearing the same clothes) separated from each other since birth but meeting unknown to each other in early manhood in the city of Ephesus. These episodes are, however, framed by the fate of their father, a merchant of Syracuse, who has been wrecked on the shore of Ephesus and who must now suffer under the laws of Ephesus, which decree death for any Syracusan setting foot on Ephesian soil – unless he can find the money for his ransom within a day. In the first scene he is shown as condemned to death, under this condition; and in the last scene he is shown as led out to his execution – only to be reprieved at the last moment. Thus, for all the humour of the comic foreground, one is all the time aware of the tragic fate in the background of the play, a fate that consists – not unlike that in *The Merchant* – in the execution of an innocent man according to the law of the land.

Now, in so far as Ephesus – like Venice in *The Merchant* – may be identified with London, where can we look for a parallel unjust law? Where, if not in the penal laws enacted in the Elizabethan parliaments against Catholic priests returning from Rome (or its equivalent in Europe) to England, for which they were liable to death, occasionally commuted by the royal clemency to banishment. Further, as has already been pointed out in the case of Antonio in *The Merchant*, these priests often referred to themselves as "merchants" (seeking "the pearl of great price") in letters that might be intercepted by the authorities. As for the place of execution, it is described in the last scene as "the melancholy vale,/ The place of death and sorry execution,/ Behind the ditches of the abbey here" (v.1). This may even have been the place of the first performance of *The Comedy*, in one or other of Shakespeare's early theatres, the Theatre or the Curtain, located as they were in the "liberty" of Holywell near Shoreditch, where there had been a large nunnery in pre-reformation times. It was also the place of execution for a Catholic priest, William Hartley, shortly after the failure of the Spanish Armada in 1588 – as is pointed out by the American scholar T.W. Baldwin in a book entitled *Shakespeare Adapts a Hanging* (1931).

A similarly tragic situation occurs at the beginning of *A Midsummer Night's Dream*, where the heroine Hermia is introduced as facing the death penalty, according to the law of Athens, for refusing to obey her father in his choice of a suitor for her, since her love is for another man. In much the same way, Catholic priests in England incurred the death penalty for their refusal to obey the law of the land, owing to their greater love of Christ and the Church. Then, just as Hermia flees with Lysander to the forest outside Athens to the secret house of his aunt, so Catholic priests took refuge in disguised sort in various country houses of the Catholic gentry – though they were always in danger from informers, just as Helena, hearing about the matter from Hermia, immediately passes on the information to Lysander's rival Demetrius.

Here we may note how Hermia is offered a choice by Theseus, as Duke of Athens, between the rigour of the law and a life of chastity spent in a convent of Diana – which reflects the situation of not a few Catholic women in Elizabethan England, who found refuge in nunneries founded for this purpose in the Low Countries, such as the well-known English Convent at Bruges connected with the descendants of Sir Thomas More. Not only in this play, but also in the contemporary *Romeo and Juliet* we may recall the proposal made by Friar Laurence to Juliet on finding Romeo's dead body in the tomb, "I'll dispose of thee/ Among a sisterhood of holy nuns." (v.3) The same expedient occurs to the mind of his fellow Friar Francis in *Much Ado About Nothing*, in case his plan for the wronged Hero proves a failure: namely, to conceal her "in some reclusive and religious life" (iv.1). Again, this is the recommendation made by the deposed King Richard to his poor Queen Isabella, as he meets her on his way to the Tower (as though following in the future footsteps of Sir Thomas More),

"Hie thee to France,/ And cloister thee in some religious house:/ Our holy lives must win a new world's crown." (v.1)

So now let us turn to *As You Like It* as a sequel to *The Merchant of Venice* among the mature comedies, with Rosalind in Arden following upon Portia in Belmont. It is a play commonly dated 1599, coinciding with the opening of the new Globe Theatre, whose motto *"Totus mundus agit histrionem"* (from Petronius) is echoed in the famous speech of Jaques on "The Seven Ages of Man": "All the world's a stage" (ii.7). The setting for most of the play is the Forest of Arden, commonly identified according to Lodge's original story of *Rosalynde* (1590) with the Ardennes in the Low Countries (where many Catholics had gone into exile from the beginning of Elizabeth's reign), but evidently associated in Shakespeare's mind with the Forest of Arden near his native Stratford and the maiden name of his own mother Mary Arden, one of the oldest and noblest names in the County of Warwick. This setting, as a place of exile for the elder Duke and his loving lords, is contrasted with the court now occupied by his usurping younger brother Frederick – just as in *The Merchant* Portia's home in Belmont across the sea is contrasted with the city of Venice.

Here, too, as in *The Comedy of Errors* and *A Midsummer Night's Dream* as well as *The Merchant*, we are faced with the threat of death as the alternative to banishment, not according to the law of the land but (in Rosalind's case) by decree of the Duke and (in Orlando's case) by the plot of his brother Oliver acting in subordination to the Duke. From the beginning of the play, the situation of the former Duke, deposed and in exile, clearly corresponds in Elizabethan terms to that of the Catholic exiles in the Low Countries, especially in the city of Louvain, and subsequently in Northern France, under the protection of the Duke of Guise, in Rome, under the protection of the Pope, and in Spain, under the protection of King Philip II. It is a situation that significantly recurs in Shakespeare's early plays: in *Two Gentlemen of Verona*, where Valentine and Silvia take refuge in the forest outside Mantua (v.3-4); in *Romeo and Juliet*, where Romeo is banished and likewise takes refuge in Mantua; and in *Richard II*, where Bolingbroke bitterly complains (like Romeo) of his banishment from England (i.3), only to turn the tables on Richard by deposing and imprisoning him at the end of the play.

In *As You Like It* the situation of the exiles is first described by Charles, the Duke's wrestler, in his conversation with Oliver:

> The old duke is banished by his younger brother the new duke; and three or four loving lords have put themselves into voluntary exile with him, whose lands and revenues enrich the new duke . . . They say he is already in the Forest of Arden, and a many merry men with him, and there they live like the old Robin Hood of England. They say many young gentlemen flock to him every day and fleet the time carelessly, as they did in the golden world. (i.1)

Such precisely was the situation of Charles Neville, Earl of Westmoreland, when on the failure of the rising of the Northern Earls which he had led with Thomas Percy, Earl of Northumberland in 1569, he withdrew to Louvain in the Low

Countries, before making his way to Rome. Such was also the situation of William Allen, formerly principal of St. Mary's Hall, Oxford, and subsequently founder of the English College at Douai in 1568 and created cardinal in 1587, generally recognized as leader of the English Catholics. As president of the English College, first at Douai and later at Rheims, and founder of its offshoot at Rome, he gathered many young Catholic gentlemen from England as students, many of whom returned to their country as seminary priests and not a few of whom suffered martyrdom. At least, in their land of exile they could enjoy freedom and even "fleet the time carelessly" – as Celia remarks on accompanying Rosalind into banishment, "Now go we in content/ To liberty and not to banishment" (i.3), with a significant echo of Kent's remark in *King Lear*, "Freedom lives hence, and banishment is here." (i.2)

So the scene shifts in the beginning of Act II from the court to the forest, where the situation of the exiles is presented by the elder Duke himself. Though the season is winter and they are living perforce in the open – "Blow, blow, thou winter wind" – he is not at all pessimistic but skilful (as his lord Amiens observes) in translating "the stubbornness of fortune" into sweetness. In contrast to the "painted pomp" and "peril" of "the envious court", all they have to endure is "but the penalty of Adam", which, seen from the viewpoint of the great Catholic classic, *The Imitation of Christ* by Thomas À Kempis, reveals how "sweet are the uses of adversity" (cf. *Imitation* I xii: *"De Utilitate Adversitatis"*). Above all, he points out, in much the same spirit as Friar Laurence in *Romeo and Juliet* (ii.3), how "this our life, exempt from public haunt,/ Finds tongues in trees, books in the running brooks,/ Sermons in stones, and good in everything." As for these "sermons in stones", they may be found not far from Shakespeare's Forest of Arden, at Wroxhall Abbey with its "bare ruined choirs" (Sonnet 73), where among the nuns before its dissolution under Henry VIII are listed no fewer than two Shakespeares, Joan and Isabella – the latter of whom may have given her name to the novice Isabella, heroine of *Measure for Measure*.

As for the sentence of banishment, pronounced by the new duke against Rosalind, as daughter of the old duke, after she has been allowed to remain at court to keep company with his own daughter Celia: when she protests her innocence, "Never so much as in a thought unborn/ Did I offend your highness" – a protest made not infrequently by the Catholic priests at their trial for treason – the duke responds:

> Thus do all traitors:
> If their purgation did consist in words,
> They are as innocent as grace itself. (i.3)

His words may be heard as echoing the accusation brought by Lord Burghley himself against the priests in his self-justifying book on *The Execution of Justice in England* (1583):

> It hath been in all ages and in all countries a common usage of all offenders ... to make defence of their lewd and unlawful facts by untruths and by colouring and covering their deeds.

It was, moreover, no less a person than William Allen who wrote in answer to Burghley's accusations of treason his other book entitled *A True, Sincere and Modest Defence of English Catholics* (1584), in which he declares "how unjustly the Protestants do charge Catholics with treason". Such is also another, anonymous Catholic complaint against the Elizabethan judges: "It is ordinary with them to call Catholics traitors". And such, we may add, is the implicit protest Shakespeare also puts into the mouth of his Duke of York in *Richard II*: "The traitor lives: the true man's put to death." (v.3)

Turning now from the introductory words of the elder duke to the various episodes that follow on one another so fleetingly in the Forest of Arden, we may note, not only – with Edward Armstrong, in his *Shakespeare's Imagination* (1946) – how frequent are the "religious references" in *As You Like It* (p.125), but also how many of these references bear on the plight of Elizabethan Catholics both abroad and in England. First, when Orlando in flight from the peril of his brother's plots arrives in the forest and comes upon the duke with his followers, he appeals to them in terms that may well have recalled the nostalgic days of pre-Elizabethan England:

If ever you have looked on better days,
If ever been where bells have toll'd to church (ii.7)

– an appeal to which the duke responds both affirmatively and repetitively:

True is it that we have seen better days,
And have with holy bell been knoll'd to church.

29

Secondly, as for the satirical character of Jaques among the duke's followers in the forest, he is sometimes identified with Ben Jonson, who had recently been befriended by Shakespeare and introduced to the Chamberlain's Men on his release from prison in 1598. It was indeed this company that produced his first play, *Every Man in His Humour*, in that very year, with Shakespeare's name heading the list of actors on the programme. And it was also from this time, only a year or two before the production of *As You Like It*, that Jonson proclaimed himself – more clearly than Shakespeare himself ever did – a Catholic recusant, and so he remained for twelve years, till he incurred some danger owing to his connection with the Gunpowder Plot.

Thirdly, Rosalind refers to the advice of "an old religious uncle of mine", in devising her plan to cure Orlando of his love, and she adds that its effect was to make the lover "forswear the full stream of the world, and to live in a nook merely monastic" (iii.2). This may recall another religious uncle who appears in *Two Gentlemen of Verona*, the brother of Proteus' father Antonio, who also from his "cloister" gives advice to his nephew to gain experience of the world. It also looks forward to yet another "old religious man" in this play, who may have come out of Shakespeare's memory of an old Marian priest, John Frith, in the village of Temple Grafton near Stratford. It is even suggested that this priest, who remained unmolested by the authorities in view of his old age, may have performed the wedding for William and Anne in 1582; and that his known skill in healing may be echoed in the character of Friar Laurence.

Fourthly, in contrast to these "old religious men" who are somehow lurking on the outskirts of the forest, there appears a "hedge-priest", Sir Oliver Martext, to perform the wedding ceremony for Touchstone and Audrey – though the former is sure that such a ceremony is invalid. He is n o Marian priest, to judge from his name, but a Puritan parson such as were commonly intruded into Elizabethan churches by the Protestant bishops to take the place of the Marian clergy. In Shakespeare's time, the name of Martin Marprelate was a fairly recent memory from the notorious Marprelate tracts, secretly printed and disseminated from a Puritan press in 1588-89; while in answer to him the Anglican bishop Thomas Cooper had published *An Admonition to the People of England* (1589), extending his chosen pseudonym to "Mar-prince, Mar-state, Mar-law, Mar-magistrate and all together". As for the precise addition of "-text", it seems to come from Bassanio's reflections before making his choice among the three caskets, in which he takes "religion" as a sphere where "the outward shows (may) be least themselves": "What damned error but some sober brow" – and what brow was there in Elizabethan times more sober than the Puritan? – "will bless it and approve it with a text?" – and who more ready to come forward with a text than the Puritan? (iii.2) From Antonio, too, it may have come, as he comments o n Shylock, the Jew-Puritan, "The devil can quote scripture for his purpose." (i.3)

Fifthly, in the Forest of Arden there is a strange power of bringing about conversions, which cluster towards the close of the play. First, there is the conversion of Orlando's wicked brother Oliver, who comes in the new duke's name to arrest Orlando, but on finding his life saved by Orlando, he is converted and so turned into a convenient partner for Celia. Thus, as he declares, "my conversion so sweetly tastes" (iv.3). Then, even stranger is the conversion of the usurping duke, who pursues his brother into the forest with an army in order "to put him to the sword"; but there, "meeting with an old religious man,/ After some question with him, was converted", and so "put on a religious life" (v.4). It is altogether incredible; but the dramatist, it seems, having come to the end of his play, doesn't care any more for probability. Lastly, Jaques, on hearing this story, resolves to go to him, considering that "out of these convertites/ There is much matter to be heard and learn'd".

So we come to the happy ending of the comedy, according to Shakespearian custom, not just in one but in three or even four marriages. In addition to Orlando and Rosalind, we have Oliver and Celia, Silvius and Phoebe, and (it seems) Touchstone and Audrey. Only, what is unusual about the wedding, given the Christian context of the play, with so many religious references in the words and so many religious men lurking in the forest, is that it seems to be a pagan ceremony performed by Hymen, "the god of every town" who further invokes "great Juno" in his function. Needless to say, he is not a real deity but one of the lords masked as Hymen, in contrast to the fairies in *A Midsummer Night's Dream* who come in at the end to bless the bridal chamber "with this field-dew consecrate", but closer to the spirits in *The Tempest* who present their masque for the engagement of Ferdinand and Miranda under the guise of Iris, Ceres and Juno.

Yet we may note that the opening words of Hymen are not pagan but Christian words, as he proclaims: "Then is there mirth in heaven/ When earthly things made even/ Atone together" (v.4). Here one is clearly reminded of the words of Christ: "There shall be joy in heaven over one sinner that repenteth." (Luke xv.7) As for the blessing of the bridal chamber by the fairies in *A Midsummer Night's Dream*, the "field-dew consecrate" clearly corresponds to the Catholic use of holy water, which had been prohibited by the Protestant authorities as superstitious; and the whole action of the fairies is reminiscent of the *"benedictio thalami"* in the old Sarum Rite. Thus the form of paganism may well look back to the old Catholic ceremonies of mediaeval England, which had been rejected as superstitious and next to pagan by the Protestants, but to which Shakespeare evidently looked back with nostalgia. He may well have made his own the sad "Farewell to the Fairies", a poem of the early seventeenth century, which laments the passing of the fairies with the disappearance of the "old abbeys", where "their songs were Ave-Maries" and "their dances were procession".

Hamlet

The genius of Shakespeare is to be seen partly in his freedom from the constraints of Renaissance criticism, with its narrow insistence on the grand rule of decorum, partly in his closeness to human nature, by freely mixing tragedy with comedy and comedy with tragedy. Not that he was merely aiming at originality or an assertion of independence from the rules of criticism. Rather, it was because always at the back of his mind and in the depth of his spirit he felt the plight of his fellow-countrymen in Elizabethan England. Thus in his comedies he seems to look away from his contemporary situation to classical Athens or renaissance Venice or the Ardennes in the Low Countries, as though to forget the troubles pressing on his mind at home. But he was unable to forget them: they insisted on entering into his dramatic thoughts and structure, in such a way as to impart an unsuspected layer of meaning and the very quality of maturity to these comedies.

Now, around the turn of the century, in the final days of Elizabeth's reign, we find Shakespeare turning from his mature comedies, culminating in *Twelfth Night*, to his series of great tragedies, beginning with the problem play of *Hamlet*. Here is a seemingly sudden change from bright comedy to dark tragedy within a little year, 1601-2. But it is not so sudden in reality, once we recognize the oppressive underthought in the mature comedies, prompting the dramatist to dismiss them with such depreciatory titles as "much ado about nothing", "as you like it", and "what you will" (as an alternative title for "twelfth night", in which a play is named after the day of its first performance). In such titles Shakespeare seems to be expressing his discontent at having to present mere frivolities, while his mind is concerned with much more important, urgent issues.

Now, therefore, in taking up the story of Hamlet, the dramatist finds himself at last in a position of facing up to himself and the problem lurking in the depth of his mind – as it were undergoing some psychiatric remedy. This remedy he finds in the old story derived from the mediaeval chronicle of Saxo Grammaticus and retold more recently in Belleforest's *Histoires Tragiques* (1559-80). This was a story with analogues in the yet more distant past, in the Old English *Beowulf* and in the Greek "Oresteia" of Aeschylus. Not many years before, it had been dramatised as a revenge play for Elizabethan audiences possibly by Thomas Kyd, author of *The Spanish Tragedy* (c.1589); and already Shakespeare had made the story his own by naming his eldest son Hamnet in 1585 – only to lose him tragically some eleven years later.

Now, however, in taking over this story of murder and revenge from the dark age of 11th century Denmark, Shakespeare makes it into something subtly different, by pushing the theme of revenge with its early mediaeval setting into the background and imparting to it a strangely contemporary relevance – replete with anachronism and oblivious of Renaissance decorum. This new aspect appears in the names of the *dramatis personae*, with its odd mixture of Latin, in Claudius, Polonius and Cornelius, Greek, in Laertes and Ophelia, Italian, in Horatio and Reynaldo, and Germanic, in the other names. It also appears in the university background of the play, not so much perhaps with Paris University, whose beginnings go back to the 12th century, as with the recently founded University of Wittenberg, which was new when Martin Luther became professor there in 1508. In the second scene of *Hamlet* we see Laertes granted formal permission to resume his studies at Paris, whereas Hamlet is denied a similar permission to go back to Wittenberg; and he in turn goes on to emphasize the absence of his friend Horatio from Wittenberg. Such repetition (four times) of this name of Luther's university in the second scene of the play is surely not without contemporary relevance. This all points unmistakably from the ostensible setting of the play in early mediaeval Denmark to its real setting in Elizabethan England, as Hamlet himself insists to Polonius, on the arrival of the troupe of players (yet another anachronism), "They are the brief abstracts and chronicles of the time." (ii.2)

So we may well ask about the play of *Hamlet*: To what extent may it be seen as a brief chronicle of Shakespeare's own time in England? Take the opening scene, with the sentries on guard on the castle battlements at midnight. From the outset we feel a problem, described as a sickness at the heart of the sentries, which somehow materializes with the appearance of the ghost (in so far as a ghost may be called "material"). Yet there remains a problem even after the disappearance of the ghost, a problem uttered by Marcellus in his request for information as to "why this same strict and most observant watch/ So nightly toils the subject of the land" (i.1). In terms of Elizabethan England, one might think of the preparations made to repel the Spanish Armada of 1588; but the failure of that armada was by no means the end to danger from Spain or to the need of preparation. Rather, we find the danger being impressed on the minds of Englishmen by government authorities till well on into the 1590's.

Then there is the further problem implied in the very appearance of the ghost, in the form of "the king that's dead" and indeed "the majesty of buried Denmark". His very shape is "questionable", raising doubts about his identity and his purpose in appearing at this time. At least, we feel a contrast between what he represents, coming as he does out of a buried past, and the present situation with its "wars and rumours of wars" (Matt. 24:6). This contrast is more clearly manifested in the next scene, as the chilly battlements at midnight give place to the council chamber the following morning, and we are introduced to the cheerful, efficient personality of the new king, Claudius, brother to the old king, with his new queen, Gertrude, formerly wife to the old king. We see him dealing with the military problem facing his kingdom in an efficient, diplomatic manner; and we feel that the new Denmark is in capable hands. All the while, however, there is a further contrast between this bright scene in the foreground and the shadowy prince, Hamlet, son to the old king, in the background. At length his presence is noticed by the queen his mother, who pleads with him to cast his "nighted colour" off; but her plea only prompts him to emphasize the basic contrast in his mind, a contrast that is basic to all Shakespeare's plays, that between "seems" and "is". "Seems, madam?" he exclaims, "Nay, it is: I know not seems!" (i.2)

This is no mere metaphysical contrast between seeming and being; but in the soliloquy that follows, when at last Hamlet is (as he prefers to be) alone, it is applied to the political contrast between the old and the new order of Denmark. The old order, represented by the ghost his father (though Hamlet hasn't yet heard of the ghost), is seen nostalgically in terms of the Garden of Eden, with his father compared to the sun-god Hyperion shining from above on the garden as the personification of his mother. The new order, on the other hand, is what Hamlet has just witnessed in the council chamber, represented by his uncle Claudius now married to his mother Gertrude, and what he now goes on to describe as "an unweeded garden that grows to seed" and is possessed by "things rank and gross in nature", in the way he regards Claudius. It is as if man, in his fall from original innocence, instead of being banished from Eden, has been suffered to remain, while Eden itself has become overgrown with weeds. Here, in contemporary terms, we may see Shakespeare's view of Elizabethan England, seemingly run by an efficient government, but based on the crimes of adultery and murder from the time of Henry VIII, not to mention the other crimes of sacrilege and repression. All the prince, and his creator, can do is utter his lamentation in solitude; but he can say nothing that may be overheard and reported against him, and so he concludes: "But break, my heart, for I must hold my tongue!"

As for this new order of Denmark, under the joint rule of Claudius and Gertrude, it has evidently been brought about by the diplomatic manoeuvring of Polonius, to whose son, Laertes, the new king makes the impressive declaration:

The head is not more native to the heart,
The hand more instrumental to the mouth,
Than is the throne of Denmark to thy father. (i.2)

It is Polonius who makes a point of knowing everything that is happening, no doubt through a network of spies such as Rosencrantz and Guildenstern, and who has presumably engineered the smooth transition of rule from the old Hamlet to the new Claudius, by-passing the young Hamlet, who is next in line of succession. Subsequently, it is he who chiefly incurs not so much the anger or even grudge as the contempt of the young Hamlet for "these tedious old fools" (ii.2). And his death at Hamlet's hands, though seemingly a mistake – "I took thee for thy better" (iii.4) – is a cause to the young prince not of remorse, though he eventually admits, "I do repent", but of apparent satisfaction.

When, therefore, we turn to Elizabethan England for the counterpart of Polonius, there is only one outstanding candidate, who actually assisted Elizabeth to ascend the throne of her half-sister Mary and who remained at her right hand till his death (loaded with wealth and honours) in 1598; and that is Sir William Cecil, Lord Burghley, first as secretary to the royal council and then as Lord Treasurer. The very name of Burghley seems to be echoed in the Latin form of Polonius, if disguised by the proximity of Poland to Denmark – while the change from B to P might be explained by a Welsh pronunciation (such as the dramatist parodies in Welsh characters like Fluellen in *Henry V* and Sir Hugh Evans in *The Merry Wives*).

What is more to the point is that Cecil's supreme power – even greater than that of the Queen himself, accounting for his nickname of "King Cecil" – was based on the accurate information of events which he derived from the spy-system organized by his associate Sir Francis Walsingham. It was characteristic of him, as of Polonius, to "by indirections find directions out"; and he could well make his own the boast of Polonius:

If circumstances lead me, I will find
Where truth is hid, though it were hid indeed
Within the centre. (ii.2)

He also prided himself on his worldly wisdom, based (like that of Bacon) on a Cambridge education, and issuing in a series of precepts he left for his son William strangely similar (though not published till later on) to those imparted by Polonius to his son Laertes on the latter's return to Paris University.

From this point onwards what we find in the development of the play is a contest of wits between Hamlet, who is pretending to be mad in seeking a means for revenge (or is he really mad?), and Claudius with Polonius, who are investigating the hidden causes of his madness. So both sides come to spy on each other. On his side, Hamlet uses the chance arrival of some travelling players at the castle to present a play-within-the-play, similar to the story he has heard from the ghost, as "the thing/ Wherein I'll catch the conscience of the king" (ii.2). On their side, Polonius proposes a plan for catching the conscience of Hamlet, and ascertaining whether his madness is due to "the pangs of disprized love" in Ophelia's rejection of him (at the behest of Polonius) or to some deeper cause (suspected by Claudius).

Now it is in the context of this plan that Hamlet comes into the lobby where Ophelia is waiting for him, while Claudius and Polonius are hiding behind the arras as "lawful espials" (iii.1). Now it is that Hamlet comes out with his famous soliloquy, "To be, or not to be" – though, doubtless to the surprise of those "espials", with hardly a mention of his particular problem. From the outset all is impersonal, without any use of the first person singular, till the speaker notices the presence of "the fair Ophelia" and humbly asks for a remembrance in her "orisons". All is in abstract, general terms, seemingly dictated by the opening use of the infinitives, "to be" and "not to be", "to suffer" and "to take arms", "to die" and "to sleep". At the most, there is a use of the first person plural, but in an impersonal, general sense, including all men. There is no evident reference either to Claudius (at least from what we are shown of him in the play) or to Gertrude, or even to the ghost, whose very return seems to be denied in the mention of death as "the undiscover'd country from whose bourn/ No traveller returns". At most, there is a vague implication of Ophelia in "the pangs of disprized love". What, then, we may wonder, is Hamlet talking about? And why is he talking about it, when he has so much of a more urgent, practical nature to talk about?

Once again, to answer these questions, we have to look from Hamlet to Shakespeare, and from mediaeval Denmark to Elizabethan England. Where in Shakespeare's experience may we find a closer parallel to Hamlet's problem than in the situation of those Elizabethan Catholics, especially of the upper class, who were daily presented with this agonizing dilemma: whether to go on enduring the intolerable persecution conducted against them by the government under Cecil, or to take up arms in one or other of the plots against the Queen's life, many of them contrived by government spies in order to convict the Catholics, and especially their priests, of treason. On the one hand, these priests, such as Persons and Southwell, were continually exhorting their followers to be patient under provocation – in pamphlets with such titles as *An Epistle of Comfort* (by Southwell) and *A Consolatory Letter* (both dated 1588). On the other hand, not a few young Catholic gentlemen, many of them from the neighbourhood of Warwickshire and even related to Shakespeare through the Arden family, supported the Earl of Essex in his ill-fated rebellion of 1601 – and later went on to engage in the Gunpowder Plot of 1605. As for the further reflection on "the whips and scorns of time", in all their generalized variety, this refers not so much to anything observable in Hamlet's Denmark as to almost everything (at least from a Catholic viewpoint) in Elizabethan England, as witnessed by Shakespeare himself in Sonnet 66, which begins (in the very phrase of Hamlet), "Tir'd with all these, for restful death I cry ... " – and which continues, in the following Sonnet 67, with nostalgic longing for "days long since, before these last so bad".

The upshot of all this mutual spying is that each side is convinced of the other's guilt: Hamlet, that his uncle is indeed, as the ghost has declared, guilty of his father's murder; and Claudius, that Hamlet is aware of his guilty deed and so presumably preparing a guilty revenge. So the latter re-solves to send the former away to England before he can take his revenge – though, as we see, Hamlet does have the opportunity of taking revenge on Claudius, but fails to take it, and instead takes (by seeming mistake) revenge on Polonius – as the latter is now caught hiding behind the arras in the Queen's room.

During Hamlet's absence, our attention is turned to the tragedy of Ophelia. We see her in her strangely pathetic madness, as she sings snatches of song, "How should I your true love know?" Here the answer to her question, "By his cockle hat and staff/ And his sandal shoon", has an odd reference to the custom of mediaeval pilgrims, whether to the shrine of St. James in Compostela in far-off Spain, or to the closer shrine of Our Lady in Walsingham – the latter long since destroyed, to-gether with all other shrines in England, in the reformation under Henry VIII. She also murmurs snatches of prayer, "God ha' mercy on his soul!", adding, "And of all Christian souls, I pray God!" No Protestant in Shakespeare's time would think of praying in such words, with their implication of the Catholic doctrine of Purgatory, where the souls of the faithful departed are to be helped by the prayers of the living. In such snatches, therefore, one may find the further implication of lament for the passing of Catholic England, with its pious customs of pilgrimage to the shrines of saints and of prayer for the faithful departed in Purgatory.

The same old ways of thinking and praying are to be heard in the words of the comic grave-digger, as he in his turn prays for the departed Ophelia (whose grave he is digging), "Rest her soul!" In his conversation with his fellow, he reveals an oddly universal viewpoint, fostered not so much by a Protestant reading of the Bible as by a mediaeval Catholic familiarity (from a remote childhood) with the mystery plays – looking as he does from the time of Adam, and "Adam's profession" of digging, "till doomsday", as being the terminus of his profession and the graves he makes. He may be criticized by Hamlet, both for his lack of feeling, in that "he sings at grave-making", and for his punning or equivocal answers; but these are ironically the very points for which Shakespeare is subsequently criticized: for lack of decorum in mixing comedy with tragedy (as in this very scene), and for his fatal addiction to puns and quibbles.

In this scene, moreover, while the clowns are digging Ophelia's grave, we see Hamlet's return to Denmark – an accident that he attributes no less than three times in the following scene to the hidden working of divine providence. "There's a divinity," he tells Horatio, "that shapes our ends,/ Rough-hew them how we will." (v.2) And again, "Why, even in that," he remarks on his possession of his father's signet, "was heaven ordinant." Finally, he is content to leave the outcome of his duel with Laertes in God's hands, considering that (in Christ's words, Matt. 10:29) "there's a special providence in the fall of a sparrow". So his practical conclusion is, "The readiness is all" – in other words, to be prepared for death, whenever and however it may come. In fact, it comes through his duel with Laertes, as a result of which both are slain by the poisoned rapier, Gertrude drinks the poisoned chalice, and Claudius is killed by Hamlet with both the poisoned rapier and the poisoned chalice. It hardly seems providential, but rather (as Horatio observes) a scene of "carnal, bloody and unnatural acts,/ Of accidental judgments, casual slaughters,/ Of deaths put on by cunning and forc'd cause" (v.2).

Amid all this confusion, however, it is interesting to note the dying concern of Hamlet as he confides it to his friend Horatio, to "report me and my cause aright", considering "what a wounded name,/ Things standing thus unknown, shall live behind me". Again, it might seem that this should hardly be a matter of concern for a dying man; but once it is placed in the contemporary context of Elizabethan Catholics, it was indeed a matter of concern for them that their cause should be reported aright, when it was so widely misunderstood and misreported through the constant official propaganda – a situation that has continued in official history from then till now. By contrast, once Hamlet has breathed his last, Horatio as it were anticipates his Catholic Requiem with his words, "Good-night, sweet prince,/ And flights of angels sing thee to thy rest!" – words that unmistakably echo the old Latin antiphon sung at the old Catholic Requiem: *In Paradisum deducant te angeli ... aeternam habeas requiem*" (May the angels bear thee to paradise ... and mayest thou have eternal rest).

Thus *Hamlet* is altogether a strange play: on the one hand, seemingly a revenge play with Hamlet as hero; and on the other, more of an anti-revenge play with Hamlet as anti-hero. It is no small problem in the play why Hamlet does not take revenge, why he delays it for so long, why he refrains from taking it when the opportunity offers. Then, when he eventually takes his revenge, it is

the result not of any plan on his part, but the mis-
carrying of the plan devised by Claudius. Yet this is
by no means the only, or even the most important,
problem of this play which is so full of problems.
There is also the problem about the identity of the
ghost, which is left unresolved; the problem about
Hamlet's love for Ophelia, and hers for him; and
the universal problem of man, on which Hamlet
touches from time to time, not least in his soliloquy
"To be, or not to be", which he evidently derives
from the Book of Job, perhaps by way of Mon-
taigne's Essays. Then we may also ask why there
are so many problems in the play, diverting our attention from its unity – if it has a unity. So we
have the celebrated criticism of the play by T.S.Eliot,
that it is an "artistic failure", and of the hero, that
he lacks an "objective correlative" for his emotions.
Both criticisms are, I think, valid; and both may be
explained, as I have tried to show, in the context of
the Elizabethan age. For the dramatist is thinking
not only of the particular tragedy of Hamlet in mediaeval Denmark, but of the general situation of
Catholics in Elizabethan England; and in this play
he reflects that situation more clearly than in any
previous play, while at the same time feeling more
keenly than ever before the impossibility of expressing his real thoughts – "But break, my heart, for I
must hold my tongue!" This is why the play of
Hamlet is at once so disorderly and so disoriented,
yet so deep and full of enigma, at once such a failure from an artistic viewpoint, yet such a notable
success for the box-office. More than any other
Elizabethan masterpiece in drama or literature, it
may be seen as looking back over the tragic events

of 16th century English history and lamenting the sad passing of Catholic England.

Measure for Measure

There are two plays of Shakespeare that stand out for their treatment of the theme of mercy v. (legal) justice. In each of them it is the heroine who pleads for the ideal of mercy in a court of law, against a self-righteous man who "stands for justice" and is thereby all but a villain. One of these plays, *The Merchant of Venice*, we have already considered, with the disguised Portia acting as a lawyer on behalf of the merchant Antonio, in contrast to Shylock the Jew, who (as we have seen) is "a kind of Puritan" at least for a Elizabethan audience. The other play now to be considered is *Measure for Measure*, with Isabella in her own person pleading on behalf of her brother before the "precise" or puritanical judge Angelo.

In the former case, the Catholic reference of the play was largely disguised – like Portia herself as a male lawyer in Venice. Only at Belmont she appears in her own nature, in association with prayer at monasteries and wayside crosses. But in the latter case, as with Isabella pleading before Angelo, there is much less disguise and it has even been said that *Measure for Measure* is the most openly Catholic of all Shakespeare's plays. Here in contrast to the Puritanism of Lord Angelo, who is plainly characterized as "precise" (all but a technical term for Puritans in Shakespeare's time), the heroine Isabella is presented as a postulant for the Catholic "sisterhood" of Saint Clare, and the Duke-hero is likewise portrayed as seeking admission, if only for a time, into the brotherhood of Saint Francis under the name of Friar Lodowick.

Hence it is all the more ironical that, when the second Folio of Shakespeare's plays (1632) was subjected to Jesuit censorship at the college of Valladolid in Spain in the 1640's, this was the only play to be entirely deleted as unfit for reading or performing. No doubt, the censor, Fr. William Sankey, was considering not so much its doctrinal content – in the controversy of Catholic v. Protestant – as its moral aspect, with its open treatment of the subject of lechery, concerning which the character most concerned, Isabella's brother Claudio, admits, "what but to speak of would offend again" (i.2).

The Catholic reference in *Measure for Measure* is most openly seen in the person of the principal character, the Duke whose name (given only in the *dramatis personae*) is Vincentio. From the outset he declares his intention to leave the rule of Vienna for a time in the hands of his deputy Angelo, who is charged with the task of enforcing the laws that have been neglected for many years. But in secret he remains in the guise – though not precisely the disguise – of a Franciscan friar. His professed purpose is to spy on the conduct of Angelo in his office; while at the same time he visits the prison to care for the spiritual needs of those imprisoned, as a true friar. Thus in the contrast between him and Angelo, we may note the same kind of contrast pointed out above in *The Merchant of Venice* between the merchant-priest and the Jewish Puritan. Not that, as Friar Lodowick, the Duke ever performs the function of a Catholic priest; but he seems more concerned with his spiritual duties than with his aim of spying on Angelo.

In his task of caring for the spiritual needs of those in prison, Friar Lodowick (as we may now call the Duke) is seen carrying out an activity that was particularly familiar to the Catholic priests in Elizabethan England. Not a few of them were arrested on or soon after their arrival in the country; but when they were imprisoned, they often found they could perform their spiritual tasks more freely in prison than when they were free – especially when the gaoler proved himself either negligent of his office or sympathetic with those of the old faith. In particular, we see Friar Lodowick visiting first Claudio's girl-friend Juliet, then Claudio himself in prison.

In his visit to Juliet, Lodowick is chiefly concerned about instructing her in the true nature of contrition, which (he teaches her) should be not "towards ourselves", that is, "as we stand in fear", but towards heaven and based on love. Such is the typical distinction drawn by Catholic moralists between "attrition" and "contrition"; and special emphasis was laid on it by Jesuit priests by way of preparation for receiving the sacrament of penance (which was not recognized as a sacrament by the Protestants). It may be added that, if in terms of the play Ludowick is a Franciscan friar, in contemporary terms of Elizabethan England he is rather a Jesuit, who might well have been addressed as a friar – especially in view of his profession to be of late "come from the See/ In special business from his Holiness" (the Pope). (iii.2)

Next, in his visit to Claudio, Lodowick urges him to face death without flinching, "Be absolute for death." (iii.1) As a result of his exhortation,he induces in Claudio the typically Jesuit frame of mind urged by Robert Southwell in his poems:

To sue to live, I find I seek to die,
And seeking death, find life. (iii.1)

This goes back, of course, to the exhortation of Jesus to his disciples: "He that findeth his life, shall lose it; and he that loseth his life for my sake, shall find it." (Matt. 10:39) But it is still what Southwell and other Jesuits are urging in an Elizabethan context. It is also what we find Shakespeare's other Friar Francis urging the heroine Hero in *Much Ado About Nothing* (where the hero's name is also Claudio): "Come, lady, die to live." (iv:1)

The character of the Duke as friar is brought into prominent relief in association with the odd, and oddly superfluous, minor character of Lucio. On the one hand, the friar is notably busy with schemes in the interests of others, and in this respect he might well be called "polypragmon" – as the Jesuit Robert Persons was called by his adversaries, not least from among his fellow-priests in the abusive Archpriest controversy of that time. On the other hand, with all his work for good, he is persistently slandered by Lucio, who calls him among other names "the fantastical duke of dark corners" (iv.3) – reminiscent of the way Burghley criticizes the Jesuits in his *Execution of Justice* for their "secret lurkings". The bare-faced manner of his slandering, and his self-portrayal as "a kind of burr" (iv.3) recall such disreputable spies as John Nichols and the dramatist Anthony Munday, who both passed themselves off as students at the English College, Rome, and went on to publish books on their experiences of Roman life.

No less clear is the Catholic connection of the heroine Isabella, sister to the Claudio who is accused of the crime of fornication with his intended bride Juliet. From her first appearance in the play she is shown as about to make her formal entry into a religious cloister of "the sisterhood, the votarists of Saint Clare" (i.4). Thus she is not exactly a nun, or even a novice, but a postulant; and her order is appropriately that of St. Clare, corresponding to the order of Friar Lodowick, that of St. Francis. It is, moreover, worthy of note that neither order appears in the source-play, George Whetstone's *Promos and Cassandra* (1578), any more than the names of hero and heroine; but they are entirely the invention of Shakespeare. As for the name of Isabella, it is not without significance that an Isabel Shakespeare is recorded as having been prioress of Wroxhall Abbey, some twelve miles to the north of Stratford – a neighbourhood to which Shakespeare's ancestry has been traced.

Out of charity for her condemned brother, Isabella consents to leave the convent for a time in order to plead for mercy on him before the unyielding judge, Lord Angelo. Then her plea is presented in much the same terms as that of Portia for Antonio in *The Merchant of Venice*:

No ceremony that to great ones 'longs,
Not the king's crown, nor the deputed sword,
The marshal's truncheon, nor the judge's robe,
Become them with one half so good a grace
As mercy does . . .   (ii.2)

This is indeed, though coming so close to the beginning, the dramatic climax of the play; but, unlike the trial-scene in *The Merchant of Venice,* it is balanced by another climax and another trial-scene towards the end. On the return of the Duke in his own form, Isabella first pleads with him for justice against Angelo – not the rigid legal justice depending on a precise interpretation of the law, as observed by Angelo himself and Shylock, but right dealing with the unjustly oppressed, namely herself and Mariana. Her claim is for the justice claimed by Christ in the Sermon on the Mount: "Blessed are they who hunger and thirst after righteousness (justice); for they shall be filled." (Matt. 5:6) And, one might add, it is the very meaning of justice for which the oppressed Catholics in Elizabethan England were clamouring, not least about the time this play was first presented at court in 1604, soon after the accession of King James I, the son of the Catholic Mary Stuart.

In this latter climax, moreover, Isabella goes on to plead, at Mariana's entreaty and in spite of the Duke's severe warning, for mercy even on Angelo himself, who has now been exposed in all his hypocrisy and accordingly condemned to death. She pleads for him, while believing that his unjust sentence against her brother Claudio has been duly carried out, and her brother is dead. Thus she appears as a very incarnation of divine Mercy, one in whom the seeming opposites of Mercy and Justice come together, as two of the four daughters of God who feature in Psalm 85 and in the mediaeval morality play of *The Castle of Perseverance.*

Not infrequently Isabella is compared with Lord Angelo for her insistence on the virtue of chastity, which she will not sacrifice even at the pleading of her brother. Rather, she is so angry with her brother at his daring to make such a plea, she quite loses her temper, saying, "Take my defiance;/ Die, perish!" (iii.1) Yet there is a basic difference between the attitude of Angelo and that of Isabella. From the outset, though described as "a man whose blood/ Is very snow-broth" (i.4), Angelo is seen as a hypocrite, one of "our seemers" (i.3); and this suspicion of the Duke is soon confirmed when Angelo yields to his desire for Isabella, while yet regarding himself in the very act of yielding as "a saint" (ii.2). Moreover, in pursuit of his desire he is shown not just as giving way to a momentary passion but as carrying it out in a cold, calculating, even Machiavellian manner – along with a readiness to lie and even to kill in order to cover up what he has done. Isabella, on the other hand, is fully genuine in her chastity, which is even proved by the way she flies into a temper with her brother when he pleads with her to accept the judge's unjust condition. If she is to be termed "Puritan" for her insistence on the virtue of chastity, it may perhaps be termed rather "Puritano-papism" – of which the Jesuits were charged in the Latin book by the Regius professor of divinity at Oxford, Laurence Humphrey, *Iesuitismi Pars Secunda: Puritano-papismi* (1584).

As for the third main character in the play, the unjust judge Lord Angelo, he is (as we have seen) comparable to Shylock in *The Merchant of Venice* for his insistence on the letter of the law; and even more obviously than Shylock, he is presented as a Puritan, especially in his characterization as "precise" (i.3) – which (as we have seen) in

Shakespeare's time was almost a fixed term for a Puritan, one of "the precise brethren". This is also the probable meaning of the unique word, or *hapax legomenon*, which is twice applied to Angelo by Claudio and Isabella in the same scene (iii.1):

> Claudio. The prenzie Angelo?
> Isabella. O, 'tis the cunning livery of hell,
>   The damned'st body to invest and cover
>   In prenzie guards!

– where one might compare Isabella's words with those of Bassanio, who also seems to have a Puritan preacher in mind:

>   In religion,
> What damned error, but some sober brow
> Will bless it and approve it with a text,
> Hiding the grossness with a fair ornament?
>   (*Merchant* iii.2)

Particularly when we go on to witness the contrast between the outward seeming of virtue in the judge and his inner corruption of vice, the very vice he is condemning in another, we find in him a parallel to the Pharisees as (in the words of Jesus) "whited sepulchres, which indeed appear beautiful outward, but are within full of dead men's bones" (Matt. 23:27). And such is the typical vice of the Puritan hypocrite, as seen by the Elizabethans.

Nor is this the first occasion for Angelo to fall into sin, though perhaps his first sin of lechery; but already he is shown as having fallen into the other sin of avarice – in which he is also comparable to Shylock. For such was the reason for his reneging on the pre-contract he had made with Mariana, as he himself informs us at the end:

> Partly for that her promised proportions
> Came short of composition.   (v.1)

– namely, Mariana's inability to pay the full sum of her promised dowry. This may remind us of the way the Puritans were described, by the Dean of Exeter, Matthew Sutcliffe, as "hard-hearted", and as "pettifoggers and scribes", who "so skin the poor, and help them not" (in *Answer to a Certain Libel*, 1592). It may also remind us of the behaviour of another Puritan, Malvolio in *Twelfth Night*, where the Captain who rescued Viola from shipwreck is said to be "in durance at Malvolio's suit", no doubt for debt (v.1).

What is, however, most Puritanical in Angelo's attitude is his extreme emphasis on the Old Law of Vienna, which includes – as did the Law of Moses – the penalty of death for the crime of adultery; though the sin of Claudio with Juliet is more exactly to be named "simple fornication", which is further attenuated by the pre-contract that merely lacks the denunciation "of outward order" (i.2). Such indeed was the characteristic of the Puritans, represented by their leader Thomas Cartwright, who in his controversy against the Anglican John Whitgift maintains that the judicial laws of Moses concerning the death penalty on idolatry, blasphemy, murder and adultery "cannot be changed"; and, he adds, "If this be bloody and extreme, I am content to be so counted with the Holy Ghost." (*Second Reply* to Whitgift, 1575) His adamant attitude may be explained by Luther's insistence on the

Bible alone as containing the pure and unadulterated Word of God, without allowing for the mild interpretation of the Church in the time of the New Testament.

By contrast to Angelo's rigid adherence to the letter of the law, which merely kills (as St. Paul says, II Cor. 3:6), Isabella (like Portia) takes her stand on the New Law of Mercy. And such was precisely the plea of Catholics in Elizabethan England, not least to the Queen herself in view (as Southwell emphasizes in his *Humble Supplication*, 1600) of her known clemency, against their chief persecutors, the Puritans. Such, too, became their yet more insistent plea to her successor on the English throne, James Stuart, who from the time of his accession was regarded as likely to grant them a respite from persecution, if only in memory of his Catholic mother. Accordingly, in the years 1603-4 they presented him with a series of petitions and supplications, which were promptly attacked by Protestant writers.

Here we may see the context in which the play of *Measure for Measure* was conceived and composed by Shakespeare, as (in the common opinion of scholars) the first play of the new reign, which was probably presented at court before the new King James I in 1604. Before, it may have been dangerous to present too obviously "Papist" a play before Queen Elizabeth; and so in *The Merchant of Venice* the real issues are disguised and the emphasis is laid on the moral ideal of "mercy" in a Jewish-Christian context. But now in the new reign the dramatist may have felt it possible and even necessary for him to be more explicit in presenting the contrast of Papist and Puritan in *Measure for Meas-*

ure. And the opinion of some scholars is not altogether far-fetched, when they see in the person of Duke Vincentio a possible reference to the new king, who might well have applied to himself words of the Duke: "I love the people,/ But do not like to stage me to their eyes", and again, "I do not relish well/ Their loud applause and Aves vehement." (i.1)

Here, too, we may see something of the complexity which the dramatist has put into the "fantastical" character of this Duke. From the opening of the play he seems to be presented, not without flattery on the part of the newly named King's Men and their dramatist, in the image of the new king himself. But then, as he takes on the habit of a friar under the name of Lodowick, he appears to resemble the habit and behaviour of the Jesuits, not least the busiest "polypragmon" of them all, Robert Persons. But there is a third likeness that emerges in him, especially from the time when the Duke is described (without slander) by Lucio:

His givings out were of an infinite distance
From his true-meant design. (i.4)

Here we may see, with not a few Shakespeare scholars, something of Shakespeare himself – though of this play, as I have indicated, what is said here is perhaps less true than of any other. Not that even in this play Shakespeare reveals "his true-meant design"; but, like Kent and Edgar in *King Lear*, he wisely, if tragically, maintains his disguise till the end.

As for the end of *Measure for Measure*, when the Duke not only puts off his friar's habit but even makes a twice repeated proposal of marriage to Isabella – though oddly without waiting for her reply, whether of acceptance or rejection – what are we to think of it? It is indeed a puzzle for naturalistic commentators, as well as for producers, who have to decide one way or the other. But surely here we have to see the allegorical meaning implicit in the title of *Measure for Measure* (from the Sermon on the Mount, Matt. 7:2) taking over. It is the Duke himself in his proper form at the end of the play who comments on the title in riddling words:

> "An Angelo for Claudio, death for death!"
> Haste still pays haste, and leisure answers leisure,
> Like doth quit like, and Measure still for Measure.
> (v.1)

Thus as Angelo has condemned Claudio to death, he also – according to the precise terms of the Law of Moses, "An eye for an eye, and a tooth for a tooth" (Exod. 21:24) – deserves to be condemned to death. But when he is reprieved at Isabella's pleading for mercy, it is revealed that his condemnation of Claudio didn't actually take effect but the young man is – contrary to the expectation of both Isabella and Angelo himself – alive. And so the plea of Mercy is fully reconciled with the demand of Justice, according to the ideal of the Incarnation foreshadowed in Psalm 85. All this, moreover, takes place under the all-seeing eye of the Duke as a human Providence, according to Angelo's own admission:

> I perceive your Grace, like power divine,
> Hath look'd upon my passes. (v.1)

In such a context, how can one interpret the proposed marriage of the Duke and Isabella at the end as anything but symbolic? At the same time it is what one expects of a Shakespearian comedy, with its conventional happy ending (though not without a deeper meaning).

Macbeth

It is against *Hamlet* in particular that T.S. Eliot has directed his famous criticism, that the play is "an artistic failure" for its lack of unity and that the hero is in need of an "objective correlative" for an emotion in excess of factual basis. Yet he might with no less truth have directed his criticism against *Macbeth*.

In many ways, *Macbeth* may be said to follow on *Hamlet* both in its defects and in its main inspiration. It shows the same poetic power, especially in the hero's employment of soliloquy, and the same philosophical reflection on life and death. Yet it was not completed in its present form till 1606, in the immediate aftermath of the Gunpowder Plot of 1605 and the trials of the conspirators in the following year. Then it is said to have been presented at court on August 7, 1606, on the occasion of the state visit of King Christian IV of Denmark.

How, then, may it be regarded as "an artistic failure"? On the one hand, it is one of the shortest of Shakespeare's plays, apparently cut for the sake of performance before the impatient King James I, and evidently composed in haste, especially towards the end. On the other hand, there are seeming additions made by a hand not Shakespeare's, notably the scenes of Hecate and the songs of the witches that betray the influence of Thomas Middleton. His own play, *The Witch*, is dated between 1610 and 1616. Then, in addition to these interpolations, there is an unnecessarily long scene (iv.3), in which Macduff is tested by Malcolm. It is commonly cut in performance.

As a play, moreover, *Macbeth* is chiefly impressive in its beginning and its end. What stands out in the memory of spectators are the first two Acts, with Macbeth's temptation by the witches and his wife leading up to his crime of murder, and the last Act, with Lady Macbeth's sleep-walking and ensuing suicide. But the intervening Acts, with the successive murders of Banquo and Lady Macduff, are somehow less intense, though the apparition of Banquo's ghost and the visions presented by the witches to Macbeth, make a gruesome impression.

As for the lack of an "objective correlative", this may be seen partly in Macbeth's startled response to the witches' prophecies, but chiefly in the choric laments over Scotland uttered by Lennox and Ross, Malcolm and Macduff, as compared with what is actually shown of the country in the play. True, Macbeth appears to be excessively vindictive against Banquo, for the purpose of covering up his own murder of Duncan, and against Lady Macduff and her children, as a means of venting his spite on the fugitive Macduff. But these victims of his are only a few individuals compared to the whole people, who are all said to be suffering under his tyrannical rule.

This national situation, implied rather than presented in the play, may be explained – as with *Hamlet* – by turning our attention from Macbeth's Scotland (in the early 11th century, shortly after the events in Hamlet's Denmark) to Shakespeare's England. As with *Hamlet*, the very names of the *dramatis personae* encourage us to do so, particularly those of the Scottish nobles, Lennox and Ross, Menteith, Angus and Caithness, who belong rather to the Scottish court of James VI c. 1600 than to the court of Duncan c. 1140. The theory has even been proposed, though it remains no more than a conjecture, that after the failure of the Essex rebellion in 1601 and the consequent danger to themselves, many of the Chamberlain's Men found it safer to withdraw to Scotland. We know of one member, Lawrence Fletcher, who had been in Edinburgh before; and it is also a fact that James VI, on becoming James I of England in 1603, showed his royal favour to the group by designating them as the King's Men.

Further, the main theme of Macbeth's usurpation of the throne of Scotland by way of murder may be seen in parallel events in 16th century England. First, the weakness of the Tudor right to the English throne had to be shored up by the systematic liquidation of all who had a better claim, such as the noble Duke of Buckingham, executed by Henry VIII on a trumped up charge. Secondly, the claim of the same Henry VIII to supreme headship over the Church of England was an unheard of usurpation, followed up by the execution of all who refused to accept it, even those like Sir Thomas More who persisted in silence. It was soon enforced by the suppression of all abbeys and shrines in England and by the further execution of such as protested, as in the Pilgrimage of Grace. Thirdly, a similar usurpation may be seen in Elizabeth's claim not only to supreme governorship over the Church of England – as a woman, she refrained from claiming "headship" – but even to the royal succession, as being a bastard in the eyes not only of the Catholic Church but even of her royal father, who therefore excluded her from his will.

Then there is the situation of exile: as seen in the two sons of Duncan, Malcolm and Donalbain.

When on the discovery of their father's murder they wisely take refuge, the one in England and the other in Ireland; also in Macduff, when his suspicion of Macbeth's guilt prompts him to join Malcolm in his English exile. Such a situation recalls the exile of the old Duke with his "loving lords" in *As You Like It*, as well as of Romeo in *Romeo and Juliet* and of Bolingbroke in *Richard II*. It also points in contemporary terms to the exile of such Catholic nobles as the Earl of Westmoreland and of such priests as William Allen from the outset of Elizabeth's reign.

The plight of these exiles is vividly depicted in the above-mentioned scene of Macduff's meeting with Malcolm at the English court (iv.3). Their plight consists not just in their personal condition of exile but rather in their feeling for the greater suffering of those at home. Already we hear, in Lennox's words, of "this our suffering country" (iii.6), and in Ross's lament, of the cruelty of "the times, when we are traitors/ And do not know ourselves" (iv.2). Now such words become as it were a duet of lamentation between Macduff and Malcolm as first Macduff complains, "Each new morn/ New widows howl, new orphans cry, new sorrows/ Strike heaven on the face", concluding with "Bleed, bleed, poor country!", and Malcolm responds, "I think our country sinks beneath the yoke:/ It weeps, it bleeds." Then Ross enters and adds his voice to theirs: "Alas, poor country!/ Almost afraid to know itself." (iv.3)

This is precisely, in contemporary terms, the lament of Catholics in and out of Elizabethan England – as of no one else. They could see both the spiritual ruin inflicted on their country by the small

Protestant party in power, led by Sir William Cecil and (in another way) the Earl of Leicester, and the physical and mental sufferings endured by their fellow-Catholics. Their laments are echoed and re-echoed in the "recusant literature" of the age, such as Allen's *Defence of English Catholics* (1584) and Southwell's *Humble Supplication* (1600). In particular, the anonymous *Declaration of the True Causes*, now ascribed to Richard Verstegan, Persons' agent in the Low Countries (1592), refers to the "lamentable and general cries and complaints of the oppressed multitude" under the harsh rule of Cecil.

Turning now from the background to the main action of *Macbeth*, we find the first problem facing the dramatist as one of psychology: how a loyal and brave general as Macbeth appears at the beginning of the play can be changed into a cruel tyrant at the end; or more precisely, how such a man can bring himself to the committing of his first crime, the murder of King Duncan – his liege-lord, his cousin, so good a king and so kind to Macbeth in person. For the solution of this problem, it is not enough to point to the motive of ambition, against which Wolsey warns Cromwell in *Henry VIII* (iii.2). Psychologically, there has to be some diabolic temptation, evoking an atmosphere of evil to make the crime convincing; and this is provided first by the witches with their incantations and prophecies, then by Lady Macbeth with her terrible invocation of "murdering ministers" that "wait on nature's mischief" (i.5).

In particular, we may pause over the terms of this invocation:

Come, thick night,
And pall thee in the dunnest smoke of hell,
That my keen knife see not the wound it makes,
Nor heaven peep through the blanket of the dark,
To cry, "Hold, hold!"

This phrase, "the blanket of the dark", was rejected
by Dr Johnson as excessively mean and common,
but later justified by Walter Whiter in his *Specimen of a Commentary on Shakespeare* (1794). It
has specific reference to the hangings in the Elizabethan theatre, when night is indicated by covering
the roof of the stage (symbolizing the heavens) with
a blanket. Such is the reference we also find at the
beginning of *Henry VI Part I,* in Bedford's lament
for the premature death of Henry V, "Hung be the
heavens with black!" It is also appropriately used
by John Buchan in the title of his novel on the time
of the suppression of the monasteries by
Henry VIII, *The Blanket of the Dark.*

The hero is thus urged by Lady Macbeth to do
the deed, but persuaded by his reason and conscience not to do it. So when he yields to her urging, and his own fear of her, he comes to feel a deep
horror at himself both before the deed and especially after it. Then his conscience becomes hard-
ened, till he declares: "I am in blood/ Stepp'd in so
far that, should I wade no more,/ Returning were
as tedious as go o'er." (iii.4) Such was also the mind
of Henry VIII, previously one of the most pious of
English kings, but impelled to take a downward
path of revenge and rapine by his new wife Anne
Boleyn and his minister Thomas Cromwell, not
only by proclaiming himself "Supreme Head" of
the Church in England but also by doing away with
such opponents as Bishop John Fisher and Sir

Thomas More. Thus, as Thomas Stapleton observes in his life of More in *Tres Thomae* (1588), "The king's thirst for blood, once gratified, grew apace."

Even Lady Macbeth, however, shows an odd sign of conscience in her admission, while Macbeth is doing the deed,

> Had he not resembled
> My father as he slept, I had done 't. (ii.2)

In the context it is not only odd: it is altogether unnecessary. But in the circumstances of Elizabethan England, it may have arisen out of the dramatist's memory of the traumatic execution of Mary Queen of Scots in 1587 – traumatic not least to Elizabeth, who signed the death-warrant but almost immediately repented of her action, when it was too late and prompt action had been taken by Cecil, anticipating such repentance. After all, Mary was Elizabeth's cousin, as being grand-daughter to Margaret Tudor, Henry VIII's sister; and so Elizabeth was reluctant to appear in the eyes of the world responsible for her royal cousin's death, though she evidently wished her out of the way.

Now we may pass from Macbeth's deed of murder to the discovery of the deed by Macduff as he returns from the royal bedchamber as an angel of judgment:

> O horror! horror! horror! Tongue nor heart
> Cannot conceive nor name thee! . . .
> Confusion now hath made his masterpiece!
> Most sacrilegious murder hath broke ope
> The Lord's anointed temple, and stole thence
> The life o' the building. (ii.3)

These words are impressive enough with reference to the sacrilegious murder of a king, as being "the Lord's anointed" – a phrase that also occurs on the lips of Shakespeare's Richard II (iii.2) with a Biblical echo from the first Book of Samuel (24:6,10). Yet such sacrilege was all too common in Scottish history, not least in Macbeth's time. It is much more impressive when seen in the setting of Shakespeare's England, and in precise relation to the action of Henry VIII in destroying so many hundreds of sacred shrines, churches and monasteries up and down the realm of England for his selfish greed, and then in punishing all who objected to him as guilty of high treason – under a special Act of Treason pushed by him through an all too compliant Parliament. That was indeed a masterpiece of confusion and sacrilege!

Here, however, a basic objection arises against my whole thesis, in these very words, "O horror! horror! horror! Tongue nor heart/ Cannot conceive nor name thee!" For they may be shown to have a different, more recent application to the Gunpowder Plot of 1605 and the subsequent trials of the conspirators in 1606. In these words one may recognise a clear echo of certain passages in the anonymous *True and Perfect Relation of the Whole Proceedings against the late most Barbarous Traitors* which appeared in the summer of 1606. In the indictment against the conspirators we read:

> The matter now to be offered is a matter of treason; but of such horror and monstrous nature, that before now the tongue of man never delivered, the ear of man never heard, the heart of man never conceived, nor the malice of hellish or earthly devil ever practised.

68

Then in Sir Edward Coke's speech for the prosecution we find a repetition of the same sentiments:

Considering the monstrousness and continual horror of this so desperate a cause . . . neither hath the eye of man seen, nor the ear of man heard the like things to these . . . This offence is such as no man can express it.

Among the conspirators on trial chief emphasis was laid on the guilt of the Jesuit Father Henry Garnet, who was made out to have been the ringleader – though he merely heard the confession of the commonly accepted ringleader, Robert Catesby, and so was drawn in spite of himself into the plot. A specific reference to him occurs in the Porter scene, introductory to the coming of Macduff. Here the Porter imagines himself as porter of hell-gate, with various people applying to him for admission. Here, for instance, is "a farmer that hanged himself on the expectation of plenty", with possible reference to Garnet's alias of Farmer; and here, he continues, is "an equivocator, that could swear in both the scales against either scale; who committed treason enough for God's sake, yet could not equivocate to heaven" (ii.3). In the trial Garnet was found to have resorted to equivocation in previous interrogations concerning his part in the plot and the confession he had received from Robert Catesby; and though he explained the moral theory of equivocation, on which he himself had written a small treatise, his explanation did not convince the jury. Nor is it only in the Porter's speech that we hear of an "equivocator"; but later on, Macbeth utters his exasperation at "the equivocation of the fiend/ That lies like truth" (v.5).

If, then, the play of *Macbeth* was indeed presented at court on August 7, 1606, and if it contains such substantial echoes of the trials and their *Proceedings* from the summer of that year, it must have been composed at a white heat of intensity, arising no doubt from the indignation in the heart of the dramatist. At least, such is the commonly accepted view of the play among Shakespeare scholars. Only, before we join them in their view, I would warn them, in Bassanio's words, against "the seeming truth which cunning times put on / To entrap the wisest" (*Merchant of Venice* iii.2). After all, let us remember the real situation in Shakespeare's London when the Gunpowder Plot was first exposed on November 5, 1605.

Remember that Shakespeare himself, as a prominent member of the Chamberlain's Men, had been involved in their production of Richard II on the eve of the Essex rebellion (with its hint to the aging Queen of the danger of deposition), and so with the rebellion itself. Among the supporters of Essex on that occasion was a young Catholic gentleman, Robert Catesby, son to Sir William Catesby whose seat was at Lapworth not far from Stratford; and Shakespeare was himself related through his mother Mary Arden with the Catesby family. Not only was this Robert a ringleader of the new Gunpowder Plot, but he met with his associates both at the Mermaid Tavern in London (where Shakespeare used to have merry meetings with Ben Jonson and others) and in Stratford at Clopton House, as well as at Coughton Court not far from Stratford. Thus it seems not unlikely that Shakespeare was aware of what was going on, even before its exposure, if only through his friend Ben Jonson, who was more directly implicated.

Consider, too, how clumsy was the whole conspiracy, involving as it did the transport by night of so many barrels of gunpowder, and how conveniently it was exposed at the last moment so as to catch the conspirators in the act – how conveniently it occurred for the anti-Catholic propaganda machine of the government, now led by Cecil's wily son Sir Robert. But then, not so conveniently for Sir Robert Cecil, almost immediately pamphlets began to circulate indicating that it was all a government plot to cast discredit on the persecuted Catholics. After all, there had been so many bogus plots arranged by government spies under the late Queen, and this now appeared as the Plot to end plots, confusion's masterpiece!

Reflect now on the practical outcome of the Plot on the English Catholics, how it seemed to expose them as traitors, murderers on an unheard of scale. Here was indeed "the equivocation of the fiend", with reference not to the Jesuit Father Garnet, who had merely resorted to equivocation as a means of protecting himself and his associates from their persecutors, and so was more victim than villain, but to the government as led by Sir Robert Cecil, whose character has been discerned in that of Don John in Shakespeare's *Much Ado About Nothing*, "whose spirits toil in frame of villainies" (iv.1). When we read, on the one hand, the case for Father Garnet, as presented in full biographical detail by Philip Caraman in *Henry Garnet and the Gunpowder Plot* (1964), we may well sympathize with him as the principal victim of the Plot; but the more we learn about the government's hand in this and other plots, from the time of Mary Stuart on-wards, we may well wonder at the tissue of lies they put out "to entrap the wisest". As for the theory and practice of equivocation, in the sense in which it was defended by the Jesuits, including Father Garnet, we find the dramatist both condoning it in his plays and going far beyond his mentors in his readiness to allow deception in a good cause. Thus in *Measure for Measure* the Duke as Friar (in some ways suspiciously like a Jesuit) explains such a plan to outwit the machinations of Lord Angelo:

> So disguise shall by the disguis'd
> Pay with falsehood false exacting. (iii.2)

Similarly, Helena, the heroine in *All's Well That Ends Well*, resorts to such a trick of deception to win back her erring husband Bertram:

> Only in this disguise I think 't no sin
> To cozen him that would unjustly win. (iv.2)

It may be noted that both these plays were com-posed in the early years of James' reign, about the very time the dramatist was also engaged on the composition of *Macbeth*.

Thus so far from *Macbeth* being anti-Catholic or anti-Jesuit, it may be interpreted as a justification of both Catholics and Jesuits against the equivoca-tion of government anti-Catholic propaganda with its "seeming truth". Yet we have also to remember the difficult position of Shakespeare, not least in the aftermath of the Gunpowder Plot, when it would have been awkward for him to offer a chal-lenge or even an implied criticism of the govern-ment, especially in a play for presentation at court.

His problem seems to be expressed in the riddling exchange between Lennox and an unnamed Lord, when the former contrives to express his criticism of Macbeth in a way he could easily retract if he found lack of sympathy in the other:

> My former speeches have but hit your thoughts
> Which can interpret further. Only, I say,
> Things have been strangely borne. (iii.6)

His attitude is strangely similar to that of Mark Antony in his speech at Caesar's funeral. The latter says he has no wish to criticize Brutus and the rest, for they are all "honourable men", but – and he pauses, to give room for an opposite meaning to creep into his words and the feelings of his hearers. Similarly, while Shakespeare seems to be upholding the official policy and interpretation of the late Plot, he manages to imply an opposite meaning, at least for those Catholic members of his audience who have ears to hear. As for the Porter's speech, in which the criticism of Garnet is most evident, doubt has been suggested as to its authenticity. Coleridge, for one, rejected it on the grounds not of its criticism of Garnet but for its meanness of phrase, as unworthy of the dramatist. But his arguments have since been set aside, owing to Thomas De Quincey's brilliant essay "On the Knocking at the Gate in *Macbeth*" (1823), which shows how aptly the speech fits into the whole dramatic context. Yet we may do well to recall Hamlet's warning against those fools who improvise without keeping to their script (iii.2), as well as the hurried way in which this play was put together – with additions by

Middleton and perhaps others – for the sudden court performance.

Now, then, let us turn to the most awkward scene, and most lengthy scene, in this shortest among Shakespeare's plays: that between Macduff and Malcolm at the English court – which is so often cut by producers of the play. Why, we may ask, is it so long? Allowing for the need of Malcolm to be on his guard, it was hardly necessary for Shakespeare to have made him so garrulous about it. But its place in the play is apparent in the wider context of Elizabethan and Jacobean England, an age of severe persecution, when the Catholics went around in perpetual fear of spies, especially such as professed themselves devout Catholics. One only has to remember the case of Mary Stuart, how she could trust no one, and how once she put her trust in Anthony Babington she fell into the government trap. Such spies were not just individual informers but part of a whole network controlled by Cecil and, under him, by Walsingham and his successors; and the most dangerous among them were the so-called *"agents provocateurs"*, who not only sought information about Catholic activities but also prompted treasonable plots to bring discredit on the Catholic cause.

This is, in fact, what we find in Macbeth's Scotland, according to Shakespeare's play but not according to 11th century history. Macbeth keeps a check on all his nobles: "There's not one of them", he maintains, "but in his house/ I keep a servant fee'd." (iii.4) In the same way, Malcolm explains his seemingly excessive caution to Macduff, with the words: "Devilish Macbeth/ By many of these trains hath sought to win me/ Into his power." (iv.3) So he, too, has to resort to a kind of equivocation in order to defeat "the equivocation of the fiend" in Macbeth. Such, too, is the policy of precaution adopted by Hamlet against Claudius and Polonius; and we find a similar vein of spying, though in a more innocent manner, in *Much Ado About Nothing* (where "Nothing" has the alternative meaning of "noting", observing or spying).

And this is precisely the true nature of the Gunpowder Plot of 1605. It was a deliberate attempt of the government under Sir Robert Cecil to provoke certain rash young Catholic gentlemen, many of whom had already been implicated in the Essex Rebellion, and again in the Main and Bye Plots at the beginning of James' reign, to engage in an even larger-scale enterprise. No doubt, they were led on not just by personal enthusiasm for the cause, but rather by blackmail in view of their past record of "treason". Above all, the government aim was by using smaller fish to catch a greater one, namely to involve the Jesuit superior in England, Father Henry Garnet, and to make it appear that he was behind the whole Plot – by means of the secret of the confessional, which he was forbidden to reveal under any circumstances. Such was a truly diabolic plan, worthy of Iago himself!

Finally, we may come to the last Act with its emphasis not so much on the downfall of Macbeth as on the sleep-walking and subsequent suicide of Lady Macbeth, prompting Macbeth to utter his famous soliloquy, "Tomorrow and tomorrow and tomorrow." (v.5) Within the limits of the play this may well seem an artistic lack of balance; but in the setting of Shakespeare's England, we may ask, who is the person most clearly corresponding to Lady

Macbeth, if only from the Catholic point of view? Clearly Queen Elizabeth. She is openly described by William Allen, in *his Admonition to the Nobility and People of England*, which he had printed to coincide with the hoped for victory of the Spanish Armada in 1588, as "this Jezabel" who "for sacrilege, contempt of holy priests, rebellion against God and cruelty, doth so much resemble our Elizabeth that in most foreign countries and writings of strangers she is commonly called by the name of Jezabel". In *Macbeth*, too, the Queen is at least implicitly compared to Jezabel, in that it is she who inspires her husband to the crime of murder and usurpation, just as Jezabel inspires the king Ahab to usurp the vineyard of Naboth by means of murder (I Kings 21).

When, moreover, *Macbeth* was first presented in 1606, the death of Queen Elizabeth was a recent memory; and it was widely reported as a particularly horrible one, with the Queen refusing to go to bed for nights on end owing to the terrible nightmares she saw there – and once her apparition was seen by one of her ladies-in-waiting, while she was in her bed. So it is not unlikely that the scene of Lady Macbeth sleep-walking would have stirred these recent memories in the minds of the first audience – though there is no correspondence in fact between the suicide "by self and violent hands" attributed to Lady Macbeth and the contemporary accounts of Queen Elizabeth's end. Above all, the simple statement of Seton, "The queen, my lord, is dead", which stirs Macbeth to utter his last, despairing soliloquy, would surely have been interpreted by contemporary spectators with reference to the one Queen whose death they all remembered. In the play, the queen is called "fiend-like", by the side of "this cruel butcher", and mention is also made of their "cruel ministers", who might be identified (in the case of Queen Elizabeth) as Sir William and Sir Robert Cecil, Sir Francis Walsingham and innumerable others who served their torturing purposes.

It is not, however, on this merely negative note that the play ends; but in his concluding speech Malcolm goes on to invoke "the grace of Grace", since it is thanks to God, with the assistance of gracious England, that the tyranny of Macbeth and his Queen has been overcome and Scotland restored to harmony and peace. Thus *Macbeth*, for all its description as a "morality play of damnation" with reference to its main protagonists, isn't wholly a tragedy, since it has a happy ending for Scotland; and so it may be more aptly described as a tragi-comedy. And the play, too, for all its artistic lack of balance, may be said (in Pope's words) to "snatch a grace beyond the reach of art" – especially once we look (presumably with the dramatist himself) from the ostensible story of Macbeth and his wife to the reality of life (at least for the English Catholics) in Shakespeare's England.

King Lear

In examining the plays of Shakespeare one by one, I have a basic question at the back of my mind: How would a Catholic member of the original audience have reacted to it? What special meaning or message would he have found in it, hidden from other, Protestant members of the audience? Or if among those other members, some informer or intelligencer, on the alert for any hidden meaning, had charged the dramatist with Catholic sympathies, how would Shakespeare have responded to the accusation?

All this is, however, admittedly hypothetical. So I may well be asked: Is there any positive evidence of such a Catholic reaction? Do we find any contemporary Catholic rejoicing over the plays of Shakespeare, as upholding his increasingly forlorn cause? Do we find any of them claiming the dramatist as one of themselves? Or on the other hand, do we find any contemporary Protestant accusing the dramatist of Popery?

In fact, we do have some positive evidence on either hand, two significant items that occur in the years 1609-11 – leading up to the time of Shakespeare's farewell to the stage at the end of *The Tempest*. First, there is the recently uncovered evidence of a group of Catholic players in Yorkshire, Cholmeley's Men, presenting two of Shakespeare's plays, *King Lear* and *Pericles*, at certain recusant houses in the years 1609-10. Both these plays had recently been published in quarto, *King Lear* in 1608 and *Pericles* in 1609, and both may be seen as containing a special message for English Catholics – as remains to be considered.

Secondly, in his *History of Great Britain*, published in 1611, John Speed criticizes the Jesuit Robert Persons for having slandered the Lollard martyr, Sir John Oldcastle, as "a ruffian, a robber and a rebel", and for having taken his authority "from the stage-players". This slander appears in Persons' treatise *Of Three Conversions of England* (1603), in which Oldcastle is described as "a ruffian knight, as all England knoweth, and commonly brought in by comedians on their stages". Oddly enough, neither Speed nor Persons mentions the dramatist by name; but they are both clearly referring to the character of Sir John Falstaff (whose name had been altered from Oldcastle at the last moment) in Shakespeare's *Henry IV* plays. Anyhow, Speed expresses his indignation against "this papist and his poet", namely Persons and Shakespeare, as being "of like conscience for lies, the one ever feigning, and the other ever falsifying the truth". He even seems to imply that the two are in league with each other, not only in the *Henry IV* plays but in others as well. It may be added that Persons had just died in 1610, the year before this charge appeared in print. And shortly afterwards, Shakespeare retired to Stratford.

Turning now to *King Lear* in particular, what special meaning or message might it have had for those Catholic audiences in Yorkshire in 1609-10? On the face of it, the play merely dramatizes the old story of an ancient British king dividing his kingdom among his three daughters according to their professions of love. It is a typical fairy story, recalling that of Cinderella. It goes back to Geoffrey of Monmouth's *Historia Regum Britanniae* (12th century), which was taken up in Holinshed's

Chronicles; and so it is variously repeated in the early Elizabethan *Mirror for Magistrates* (1574), in Spenser's *Faery Queene* II x (1589), and in the source play, *King Leir and his three daughters*, which was published in 1605. In this latter play there is an evident Protestant bias, with the heroine Cordelia portrayed as a Puritan, "so sober, courteous, modest and precise", and "right fit to make a Parson's wife", and the wicked Gonorill betraying a Papist acceptance of Purgatory. In his play, however, Shakespeare removes all obvious Christian references and sets the action in an explicitly pagan background, with emphasis on the theme of "nature", though not without a deep Biblical undertone.

Outwardly, at least, just as *Hamlet* and *Macbeth* have their setting in Denmark and Scotland in the 11th century, *King Lear* is about pre-historic Britain around 700 B.C. But at a deeper level, as with *Hamlet* and *Macbeth*, so too in *King Lear* we find an undercurrent of reference to Elizabethan England, which first appears in the names. To begin with, Lear is supposed to be "King of Britain", as he is described in the *Dramatis Personae*; and yet in all the play there is surprisingly no mention of "Britain". Only the adjective "British" appears twice: in the mad song of Edgar, "I smell the blood of a British man" (iii.4), and in "the British powers" under Albany and Edmund as they march against Lear and Cordelia (iv.4). This contrasts with the frequent mention of "Britain" (over 20 times) in the subsequent play of *Cymbeline*, where the titular hero is also "King of Britain" in later, Roman times.

What, we may ask, is the reason for this odd silence? It may be that Shakespeare wishes to lay stress on the inner parallel with contemporary events in England; whereas the name of "Britain" refers both to the prehistoric past of the island and to the present union of England and Wales under the Welsh dynasty of Tudor. Such is the implication of Speed's title, *The History of Great Britain*, as it were on the side of the Tudor dynasty and government; whereas Shakespeare's omission of the name seems to point to that condition of England symbolized in what he calls (in Sonnet 73) "bare ruin'd choirs, where late the sweet birds sang".

Then, in contrast to the two ducal names of Albany (for the Celtic North) and Cornwall (for the Celtic West), we find the two earls of Kent and Gloucester endowed with Saxon names and mediaeval titles. On the other hand, there are no place-names in the whole play, apart from the town of Dover on the Kentish coast opposite France; and it is to this town (with its Saxon name) that the whole movement of the play tends from the third Act onwards. This is because the main action of the play culminates in the French invasion under Cordelia and her subsequent defeat, together with her old father, by the British forces under Albany and Edmund.

As regards the two suitors for Cordelia's hand, the King of France and the Duke of Burgundy, these regions both emerged out of the barbarian invasions at the downfall of Rome. The kingdom of the Franks (or France) was established in the early 6th century; and the duchy of Burgundy in the 9th century. Finally, as for the names of Edgar and Edmund, as well as Oswald, they are evidently Saxon. Thus, to say the least, the whole play of *King Lear* is riddled with deliberate anachronism – though none of the names (unlike *Hamlet* and *Macbeth*) point unmistakably to the 16th century.

It is, however, not so much the names as the main action of the play that points to Shakespeare's England, especially when seen from a Catholic viewpoint. Just as the movement of the play converges on Dover, culminating in the French invasion under Cordelia for the rescue of Lear: so in Shakespeare's England and the reign of Queen Elizabeth everything is seen to converge on the Narrow Seas and the expedition of the Spanish Armada in 1588. This expedition was undertaken by Philip II, partly to avenge the execution of Mary Stuart in 1587, partly to rescue the afflicted Catholics of England; and he was supported by Pope Sixtus V's Bull of Excommunication with Cardinal Allen's explicatory *Admonition to the Nobility and People of England* (1588). But as we know, this Armada was defeated partly by the English ships under Sir Francis Drake, partly by stormy weather. Two references to the Armada may be detected in words of Cordelia: first, on her arrival in Dover, proclaiming her sincere intention:

No blown ambition doth our arms incite
But love, dear love, and our ag'd father's right.
(iv.4)

and secondly, on their sad defeat in battle:

We are not the first
Who with best meaning have incurred the worst.
(v.3)

The first word seems to echo Allen's *Admonition*, justifying the Spanish invasion for religious, not political reasons; while the second seems to point to a precedent for such lamentable failure of a good cause in the Armada, in contrast to Protestant claims that God was evidently on their side.

In general, it may be noted that the good characters in *King Lear*, as in *As You Like It*, are all suffering from exile, banishment, disinheritance and persecution. The very word "persecution" is uniquely used by Shakespeare in this play, in the mouth of Edgar, though he applies it rather to the weather (ii.3). First, in the main plot, Cordelia is banished by her father for her truth; and then the Earl of Kent is also banished for his fidelity without flattery. On his departure, he echoes Celia's similar words in *As You Like It*: "Freedom lives hence, and banishment is here" (i.1), and the deposed Richard's words in *Richard II*: "He'll shape his old course in a country new" (v.1). Next, in the second plot, Edgar is forced to flee from his father's anger through Edmund's trick and to assume the disguise of a mad beggar. Kent also returns in disguise in order to serve Lear. Subsequently, both Lear and Gloucester, after having realized their deception, are driven into a kind of exile on the heath and make their separate ways to Dover – Lear in madness, Gloucester in blindness. Then in the storm that breaks over the heath all except Cordelia are involved; while it is from France that Cordelia comes to Dover to rescue them. It is all precisely, as we have seen in previous chapters, the situation of English Catholics, whether in exile abroad or at home in disguise or in prison – above all, the priests and the Jesuits.

This is a situation that is strikingly portrayed in the strange prophecy of the Fool:

> When priests are more in word than matter;
> When brewers mar their malt with water;
> When nobles are their tailors' tutors;
> No heretics burn'd but wenches' suitors . . .
> Then shall the realm of Albion
> Come to great confusion. (iii.2)

These words are an adaptation of what is called "Chaucer's prophecy" in R. Verstegan's *Declaration of the True Causes* (1592) – namely, the spurious "Plowman's Tale", that does not appear in the text of *The Canterbury Tales*. Verstegan merely implies an application of the prophecy to the contemporary state of England; but this application is made explicit in the anonymous letter of 1589 from "a Spanish Gentleman", who gives this rhyme as "the very lively portrait" of England:

> When faith faileth in priests' saws,
> And lords' hests are held for laws
> And robbery is held purchase
> And lechery is counted solace,
> Then shall the land of Albion
> Be brought to great confusion. (p. 26)

It is interesting, to say the least, how accurately the Fool's prophecy echoes the interpretation of this rhyme in contemporary recusant literature.

As for the second plot concerning the Earl of Gloucester and his two sons, Edgar and Edmund, it is derived from the other story of "The Blind King of Paphlagonia" narrated in Sidney's *Arcadia*. No doubt, the dramatist was impressed by the parallel between Lear with his three daughters and Gloucester with his two sons, involving the contrast between good and bad. Then, more precisely for the characterization of Edgar in his pretended madness, he took for his further source Samuel Harsnett's *Declaration of Egregious Popish Impostures* (1603). Harsnett was then chaplain to Richard Bancroft, Bishop of London, and he had already devoted his debunking skill to certain Puritan exorcisms in the North of England, conducted by one John Darrell. Now he turned his attention to other, Papist exorcisms that had taken place long since not far from London in the mid-1580s. These had been conducted by the Jesuit Fr William Weston (alias Edmonds) with a number of seminary priests, notably a school companion of Shakespeare's from Stratford, Robert Debdale, who had departed for the continent in 1575 with the schoolmaster Simon Hunt and joined the English seminary at Douai. Already these exorcisms seem to have been in Shakespeare's mind in his composition of the early *Comedy of Errors* in the early 1590s, where an exorcism is conducted on stage by a schoolmaster named Pinch – though the exorcist's name seems to have reference rather to a Puritan critic of the Papist exorcisms named Phinch, whose book *Knowledge or Appearance of the Church* was published in 1590. Subsequently a MS "Book of Miracles", attributed to William Weston, came into the hands of the Bishop of London, who passed it on to his chaplain as convenient material for use against the Papists; and so Harsnett's book is a detailed refutation of Weston's manuscript.

Why, we may ask, did Shakespeare use this book of Harsnett's so extensively, not only in *King Lear* but also in later plays up to *The Tempest*? This is, we may note, the first time he used a book of religious controversy for his source-material. Maybe he found Harsnett's language both vivid and theatrical, filled as it is with images from the drama. Maybe he found Harsnett's quotations of the ravings of the victims of possession appropriate for the characterization of Edgar as a mad beggar. Maybe he was specially interested in reading of the further adventures of his former school-companion, Robert Debdale (who was put to death soon after the events narrated). It has even been suggested that the dramatist was in basic agreement with the controversialist in the latter's statement of the official Anglican position on miracles and diabolic possession (that these things don't happen nowadays). This suggestion even includes the attribution of the villain's name of Edmund to Weston as Fr Edmonds, and perhaps also to his great Jesuit precursor Edmund Campion.

Anyhow, in contrast to such superficial similarities of name, there is all the difference in the world between Edmund the persecutor with his political power and the Jesuits of the Elizabethan age, who are rather to be compared with Edgar as hunted victim. When Edmund tells his brother, "Intelligence is given where you are hid"; and when Gloucester goes on to threaten to bar "all ports" against Edgar and to "send far and near" his picture as a means of identifying the culprit (ii.1); and when Edgar himself hears himself "proclaim'd", and finds "no port free, no place/ That guard and most unusual vigilance/ Does not attend my taking", and so decides to disguise himself and change his name – such was precisely the situation of Catholic priests, not least the Jesuits among them, in Elizabethan England. From Campion's pen in particular we have the following self-description in a letter he wrote to his Jesuit superior in Rome in 1580:

> I cannot long escape the hands of the heretics; the enemy have so many eyes, so many tongues, so many scouts and crafts. I am in apparel to myself very ridiculous; I often change my name also ... Threatening edicts come forth against us daily.

Among such edicts were the two royal proclamations issued, in the Queen's name, but no doubt penned by Lord Burghley, dated July 15 1580 and January 10 1581. The sea-ports on the South coast were kept under constant watch for priests arriving or leaving; and Catholic houses throughout the land were under continual surveillance by spies (or intelligencers) and informers. If then there is anything in the suggested attribution of Edmund's name to Campion, it may be explained as a "blind" to distract the attention of possible spies in Shakespeare's audience.

There is indeed something holy about Edgar, no less than about Cordelia. It is by no means inappropriate that in the BBC production of *King Lear* Edgar was presented as an image of the suffering Christ, wearing a crown of thorns, rather as in the famous painting of "Ecce Homo" by Guido Reni. For it is his aim to save the mind and the soul of his penitent father Gloucester. It is he rather than his brother Edmund who resembles Edmund Campion if not Fr Edmonds.

By the way, this state of division within families, which seems so "unnatural" (in the strict sense of the word as used in the play) was by no means uncommon in Elizabethan England, where it was all too often brought about by differences in religion – or rather by differences between a religious conscience and the lack of it. Shakespeare himself might have observed such differences in his mother's Arden family or in the related Throckmorton family, where there was a Protestant branch (favoured by the state) and a Catholic one (ruthlessly discriminated against). He might also have known the case of the recusant family of Fitzherbert in Essex. The ambitious son of the family made a contract with the infamous torturer Richard Topcliffe, offering him £5,000 (a considerable sum of money in those days) to get his father and uncle convicted as recusants and to torture them to death, that he might succeed to his father's property. It is all too reminiscent of Edmund's behaviour. In fact, however, it was Topcliffe himself who secured the inheritance.

As for the way Edgar saves his father by leading him in imagination to the top of Dover cliff and letting him make a seemingly suicidal leap, it is somehow of a piece with the way of the friars as presented in three preceding plays. In *Romeo and Juliet* we find Friar Laurence proposing the way of apparent death as a remedy for both Romeo and Juliet. In *Much Ado About Nothing* we find Friar Francis proposing a similar remedy – with better success – to the heroine, Hero, "Come, lady, die to live." (iv.1) And in *Measure for Measure* such is also the advice given by the Duke in disguise as Friar Lodowick to the hero Claudio, "Be absolute for death." (iii.1) Such was, moreover, the constant teaching of Catholic priests in Elizabethan England to their persecuted flock, to be patient amid suffering and even death. Their words are aptly summarized by one of their number, the Jesuit martyr-poet Robert Southwell, in one of his poems:

> I live, but such a life as ever dies . . .
> Thus still I die, yet still I do revive,
> My living death by dying life is fed.

This teaching, however, isn't just the general one of accepting death as a way to life: it is also specifically directed to the example of Christ crucified, both in the moment of his death, when his side was pierced with a lance, and in the moment after death, when he was taken down from the cross and laid in the arms of his sorrowing mother, as portrayed in the *Pietà*. The former moment we find notably emphasized in the figure of Edgar, especially in the last two Acts of *King Lear*. First, he is indicated by his father Gloucester as a Messianic Man of Sorrows, recalling his previous meeting with Edgar and Lear:

> In the last night's storm I such a fellow saw,
> Which made me think a man a worm. (iv.1)

Here is an obvious echo of the Messianic Psalm 21: "I am a worm and no man" – which is often taken together with the parallel passage in Isaiah 53:3: "He is despised and rejected of men." And this is in turn reminiscent of France's words to the rejected Cordelia at the beginning of the play (i.1):

> Fairest Cordelia, that art most rich, being poor;
> Most choice, forsaken; and most lov'd, despis'd.

From now on it is Edgar who gives frequent expression to this suffering he witnesses in others. On the meeting between the mad Lear and the blinded Gloucester he exclaims, "O thou side-piercing sight!", and again, "I would not take this from report: it is,/ And my heart breaks at it." (iv.6) Then in the final Act he describes the heart-broken death of his father "Twixt two extremes of passion, joy and grief", and the subsequent heart-break of Kent, in whom "the strings of life/ Began to crack" (v.3). Thereafter we witness on stage the heart-broken end of Lear himself, at which it is Kent in turn who exclaims, "Break, heart; I prithee, break!" This all seems to constitute a dramatic representation of the piercing of Christ's side on the cross (John 19); while the subsequent scene of the *Pietà* is represented when Lear, as sorrowing father, comes on stage bearing the dead body of his innocent daughter. Then Albany exclaims, pointing at the scene, "O see, see!", as it were echoing the words of the lamenting Jeremiah, "Behold and see, if there be any sorrow like unto my sorrow!" (Lam. 1:12) – words applied by the Church to the sorrowing mother in the liturgy for Holy Saturday.

Here above all a Catholic audience, such as those for whom the play was enacted in North Yorkshire, might well have recognized the dramatist's deep lament for the passing of Catholic England as the outcome of the long-protracted Elizabethan persecution. At the beginning of the new reign of James I in 1603, Catholics had entertained some hopes of him, as being the son of the Catholic Mary Stuart, though he had been brought up in the Protestant religion. At least, they had hoped he might extend to them some measure of toleration, when they presented him with their petitions on his progress from Edinburgh to London. But it had been in vain. Whatever may have been James' personal desire to arrange a reconciliation between Catholics and Protestants, he was no less in the power of the great enemy of Catholics, Sir Robert Cecil, than Elizabeth had been in the power of Robert's father, Sir William Cecil. And so in the early years of James' reign the penal laws were enforced against Catholics more rigidly than ever, prompting some Catholic gentlemen to take the desperate measure of blowing up the Houses of Parliament. Then even the stern prosecutor, Sir Edward Coke, admitted that "if any one green leaf for Catholics could have been visibly discerned," they wouldn't have become so desperate. But now all hope was at an end. This is perhaps why of all Shakespeare's plays *King Lear* is so undeniably his greatest masterpiece. It is also the play of his most calculated to touch the hearts of a Catholic audience with its feeling of pity and its message of patience. This is the message preached by Edgar to his father: "Bear free and patient thoughts" (iv.6), and by Lear (who has himself learnt it from Edgar) to Gloucester: "Thou must be patient." And so we are brought to the concluding words of the play, which are fittingly ascribed by the Folio to Edgar, though by the Quarto to Albany:

The weight of this sad time we must obey;
Speak what we feel, not what we ought to say.
The oldest hath borne most: we that are young
Shall never see so much, nor live so long. (v.3)

The Winter's Tale

Of the two plays of Shakespeare presented at recusant houses in Yorkshire in 1609-10, there can be little doubt concerning the relevance of *King Lear* to the Catholic audiences there. But what about the other play of *Pericles*? Would it have had any special meaning for such audiences?

At first sight, in contrast to the masterpiece of *King Lear*, *Pericles* might seem to come as an anti-climax. It was even excluded from the first two folios of 1623 and 1632, in spite of bearing the name of Shakespeare on the title-page, and was only admitted to the third folio of 1664 almost as an appendix or after-thought. This is less surprising on consideration of the inferior quality of the first two Acts, and it is only from Act III that the master-hand of Shakespeare clearly takes over – as if he has been asked to undertake a revision of the play. But why, we may ask, did Shakespeare accept the task? Was it just to oblige his company, or a younger dramatist such as George Wilkins (whose name is commonly mentioned in this context)? Or isn't it rather because he found something in the idea or plot of the play to inspire him?

So what was the idea or plot of the play? It is a story based on John Gower's tale of "Apollonius of Tyre" in his long *Confessio Amantis*. In the play Gower himself appears from time to time under the name of "ancient Gower", as a one-man Chorus. But the name of the hero is changed from Apollonius to Pericles, partly from the character of Pyrocles in Sydney's *Arcadia*, partly because the name of Apollonius would not fit the iambic metre of blank verse. The story begins with the sad experiences of the hero as he sails the eastern Mediterranean Sea and successively loses his dear wife Thaissa in childbirth and his dear daughter Marina when she is kidnapped by pirates. In the outcome, however, contrary to all expectation, he is successively restored, thanks to the miraculous intervention of the goddess Diana, first to his long lost daughter at Miletus, then to his wife whom he has given up for dead but who turns out to be the high priestess of Diana at Ephesus. His experience is thus strangely akin to that of the old merchant Aegeon in *The Comedy of Errors*, when he also finds his long-lost wife as abbess in Ephesus.

It is precisely in this happy outcome that we may find a parallel not only with the early *Comedy of Errors*, but also with the more recent tragedy of *King Lear*. For it may be said that a basic theme of the latter play is the one enunciated by Kent, "Nothing almost sees miracles but misery" (ii.2). In contrast to the misery endured by the two old men, Lear in his madness and Gloucester in his blindness, we are shown the miracles of their blissful reunion with their good children, Lear with Cordelia (iv.7) and Gloucester with Edgar (described by the latter, v.3). Above all, Act IV sc. 7 is the culminating recognition scene, when the old king rising above his madness exclaims:

> Do not laugh at me,
> For as I am a man, I think this lady
> To be my child Cordelia.

True, this moment of bliss is followed by the bitterly sad ending of the deaths of both Cordelia and

Lear; and yet it remains in the memory as the high moment of the play.

As for *Pericles*, we are shown the misery endured in a long-drawn-out process by the hero who has (unlike Lear) lost both wife and daughter through no fault of his own except perhaps his imprudence in entrusting the little Marina to the unreliable care of Cleon and Dionyza at Tarsus. But then a double miracle occurs in Act V, first when he is reunited with his daughter Marina – as a repetition of that experienced by Lear with Cordelia – and secondly when, inspired by a dream of Diana, he goes on to Ephesus for his further reunion with his wife Thaissa, in a kind of resurrection.

Here is no sad ending, as in *King Lear*. It is rather as if the dramatist now desires to atone for the sadness at the end of *King Lear* by repeating the blissful reunion of Lear with Cordelia both in this and in the subsequent plays of *Cymbeline* and *The Winter's Tale*. Also from a Catholic viewpoint one may say that if *King Lear* is a lament for the passing of Catholic England, with only a lesson of patience by way of comfort, in those subsequent plays Shakespeare is looking from past sorrows to greater joys to come. From this viewpoint, one may add that, for all their difference in dramatic quality, *King Lear* and *Pericles* make a perfect pair. Nor need we despise the latter as altogether inferior, considering how popular it was at the time both on the stage and in printed form (the quarto was reprinted no less than six times from 1609 to 1613), and how it shows a new dramatic vision born out of suffering, a series of miracles seen amid misery.

Now we may turn at last to *The Winter's Tale*, as the third and perfect specimen of this new genre of tragi-comedy, following on *Pericles* and *Cymbeline*. Its plot is particularly similar to that of *Pericles*: in that the hero, Leontes, King of Sicilia, loses both his wife Hermione and his daughter Perdita, only to recover them both again thanks to the oracular intervention of Apollo. But in this play, unlike *Pericles*, but more like *King Lear*, the hero is grievously at fault. His very name suggests a connection with Lear; and his kingdom with its three-cornered shape (expressed in the old name of Trinacria) suggests that of England. Above all, just as Lear is angry with Cordelia for her truth and banishes her, so Leontes conceives an irrational jealousy against Hermione and puts her on trial, while banishing her new-born daughter Perdita.

So, too, in contemporary terms of sixteenth-century England, we may say that, just as in *King Lear* Shakespeare is thinking of Elizabethan England where events move up to the sailing of the Spanish Armada, so in *The Winter's Tale* he is thinking of England in the reign of Henry VIII where events centre on what More called "the king's great matter" of the divorce from Queen Katharine.

In the first half of the play we see how Leontes charges his queen with adultery, on his own mere suspicion; how he formally arraigns her in a court of law; and how she dramatically appeals to the oracle of Apollo at Delphos (in a combination of Delphi and Delos). This is exactly parallel to the behaviour of Henry VIII towards his first queen Katharine of Aragon. Not that he charges her with adultery, but in his doubt concerning the validity of their marriage (though she had duly received a dispensation from the Pope to marry her first husband's brother) he seeks a legal divorce or rather annulment of their marriage; and this leads up to the trial in which she makes her dramatic appeal to the Pope in Rome – a parallel that is all the more convincing in that Rome is sometimes compared by Protestant controversialists to the oracle of Apollo at Delphi. Then, too, in the play Hermione is shown as daughter to the Emperor of Russia (a potentate who appears on the European scene long after the oracles have ceased); while in history Katharine of Aragon is both aunt to the great Emperor Charles V and daughter to Ferdinand and Isabella of Spain.

On the occasion of the trial, Hermione's bearing is no less dignified than that of Katharine in the proceedings for the divorce, as presented in dramatic form in Shakespeare's last history play of *Henry VIII* – concerning which Dr Johnson has the famous remark that "the genius of Shakespeare comes in and goes out with Katharine". As for the oracle, it is vividly described by the Sicilian ambassadors Cleomenes and Dion, with emphasis on "how ceremonious, solemn and unearthly" the sacrifice was – as it were a Solemn High Mass in the basilica of St Peter's, Rome. As for the pagan reference here and elsewhere in this play, as in all the other tragi-comedies, it may be explained by the Act in Restraint of Abuses of Players, passed by Parliament in 1606 under Puritan influence, which made it prudent for the dramatist to provide all his plays from then onwards with a conveniently pagan background.

Another significant parallel between the play and the reign of Henry VIII may be found in the character of Camillo, as the wise counsellor to

Leontes. There is even something holy about Camillo, the way Leontes calls him "priest-like"; and he is further described by Polixenes as "a gentleman" and "clerk-like experienc'd" (i.2). He is, however, charged by Leontes with the task of poisoning Polixenes, on the mere suspicion of his adultery with Hermione; but Camillo only warns the other of his danger and flees with him to the kingdom of Bohemia. In him we may find a certain parallel with the wise counsellor of Henry VIII, Sir Thomas More, who also appears in the figure of the wise old Gonzalo in *The Tempest* with his ideal commonwealth and love of "merry fooling". For More likewise refused to recognise the divorce from Queen Katharine or the accompanying separation from Rome; though instead of taking refuge from England, as so many Catholic exiles did in the early years of Queen Elizabeth, he suffered imprisonment in the Tower followed by execution in 1535.

As for the character of Polixenes, King of Bohemia, who is so unjustly accused by Leontes of trifling with the queen: first, we may note how Shakespeare has strangely interchanged the two kingdoms in the source, Robert Greene's *Pandosto*, so as to make his distempered hero ruler over the island kingdom of Sicilia – and thus akin to England – while relegating his rival to the inland kingdom of Bohemia. Thus Bohemia may be seen as corresponding, like Belmont in *The Merchant of Venice* and the Forest of Arden in *As You Like It*, to the Catholic continent. What is more, we find Polixenes (with his name signifying "many guests") described in strangely papal terms by the repentant Leontes, in his words of welcome to Prince Florizel:

You have a holy father,
A graceful gentleman, against whose person,
So sacred as it is, I have done sin.   (v.1)

Certainly against the sacred person of the Pope,
Henry VIII may well be described as having "done
sin". A similarly papal reference may be found in
the preceding play of *Cymbeline*, where the king of
Britain, misled by his second wife, banishes his
daughter's newly married husband Posthumus, and
the latter takes up his residence in Rome. There he
is oddly described as sitting

among men like a descended god:
He hath a kind of honour sets him off,
More than a mortal seeming . . . a sir so rare,
Which you know cannot err.   (i.6)

Thus if Cymbeline corresponds to Henry VIII, his
second wife would be Anne Boleyn, and Imogen,
his daughter by his first wife, would be Mary Tudor;
and then the loyalty of Imogen to Posthumus may
be compared to that of Mary to the Pope in Rome.
At least, it is an interesting set of correspondences,
not without a wise old counsellor, Belarius.

All this, however, corresponds to the
negative or tragic part of the tragi-comedy, with the
trial of Hermione corresponding to that of
Katharine of Aragon in the England of Henry VIII.
But now we have to turn to the positive or comic
part from Act IV onwards, introduced by Time as
Chorus proclaiming the passing of sixteen years.
Here we also turn from the tragic action in Sicilia,
as being the location of court or city, to the
countryside of Bohemia – corresponding in

98

contemporary terms to the contrast of London/ Westminster and the Catholic continent. So, too, we return from the tragedy of Hermione, the former queen, who has been given out as dead since the time the oracle was proclaimed in the law-court, to the comedy of Perdita now introduced as queen and mistress of the sheep-shearing feast. Her very name suggests the grace of her that has been lost (in Latin, *perdita*) through his own folly, and an interesting parallel with Lear, who is called "poor perdu" (iv.7) – lost, like the Prodigal Son, but fortunately found again. Now she is courted by Prince Florizel, son of Polixenes; and now they both incur the anger of the old king, Polixenes, and so they make their way – on Camillo's shrewd advice – to Sicilia. Now they are warmly welcomed by the repentant Leontes to Sicilia "as is the spring to the earth" (v.1); and as the identity of Perdita is realised, there follows a series of recognition scenes recalling that of Lear with Cordelia, that of Pericles with Marina and that of Cymbeline with Imogen.

Then in the climax of the play, all are led by the loyal Paulina, the former handmaid of Hermione, to a new "statue" of Hermione – said to have been made "by that rare Italian master, Julio Romano", famous for his connection with Raphael and the paintings at the Vatican. In fact, it turns out to be no statue but the living reality of Hermione, in a miracle of resurrection similar to that by which Thaissa was resuscitated and eventually restored to the sad Pericles. It is on this occasion that Paulina insists to Leontes and Perdita, "It is requir'd/ You do awake your faith"; and then she addresses the statue:

Bequeath to death your numbness, for from him
Dear life redeems you.   (v.3)

Again, the explicit setting is all pagan; but the deeper implications are all Christian, even theologically so – with a theology of grace and repentance.

Here we have not just the painful lesson of patience, as taught by Edgar to Lear and Gloucester in that play, but a more positive exhortation to faith and hope of new life. There is even an expectation of miracles, even the miracle of resurrection, which is not so much Anglican – with their characteristic assertion that "the age of miracles has ceased" – as Catholic. In this connection we may note two things. The first is how all these plays, from *King Lear* (and the contemporary comedy of *All's Well That Ends Well*) onwards, seem to insist on miracles. Indeed, behind most of them – as R.G. Hunter has shown in his study on *Shakespeare and the Comedy of Forgiveness* (1965) – may be recognised the influence of the late mediaeval miracle plays, such as the play of St. Helena in *All's Well*, the play of St. Mary Magdalen in *Pericles*, and two miracle plays of the Virgin Mary, *Ostes Roy d'Espagne* in *Cymbeline* and *Miracle de l'Emperis* in *The Winter's Tale*. This was, moreover, a tradition still maintained by the Jesuit drama in Europe, though it had been killed in Post-Reformation England.

The second point to notice is that even at this time a controversy was being waged between Catholics and Protestants over certain miracles attributed to the Virgin Mary at her shrine of Montaigu in Brabant, near Brussels. They were

100

proposed and defended by Catholic authors from 1604 onwards, but attacked by Protestants in the Low Countries and England according to their teaching that "the age of miracles has ceased". To this controversy Shakespeare himself seems to allude in *All's Well That Ends Well*, when the heroine Helena uses a recipe left her by her dead father to cure the King of France. Then the Lord Lafeu comments sarcastically on those who "say miracles are past", and points to this "showing of heavenly effect in an earthly actor", recognising as he does "in a most weak and debile minister, great power, great transcendence" (iii.3). This theme of miracles, which may be traced as far back in Shakespeare's drama as *The Comedy of Errors*, may be said to culminate in the supreme miracle of Hermione's resurrection – however much the dramatist may furnish it with a far-fetched "natural" explanation. From a Catholic viewpoint, it may point to the conclusion not so much that "the Catholic cause is lost" as that "the Catholic cause can now be saved only by a miracle".

Finally, with the movement in plays like *The Winter's Tale*, we may turn with the dramatist himself from the theatrical world of London to the peace of his family life in the countryside round Stratford. There he may well have directed his thoughts – like the heroes of his last plays – not so much to his wife Anne as to his dear daughter Susanna. Already in 1606 her name had strangely appeared on a recusancy list, when the authorities were rounding up suspected Catholics in the immediate aftermath of the Gunpowder Plot. And in this respect she was following in the footsteps of her grandfather John Shakespeare, whose name had also appeared on such a list in 1592 at the height of a series of financial misfortunes. But then in the following year 1607 she married the respectable Dr John Hall, whose Anglicanism is attested by his support of the church of the Holy Trinity in Stratford, but whose medical practice included several Catholics of the district. The year after that, 1608, Shakespeare's Catholic mother Mary Arden died. Lastly, it was the turn of Shakespeare himself to die, after five or six years of self-imposed exile in Stratford – or didn't he rather regard it, with Celia and Kent, as liberty not banishment? – in the year 1616. Concerning the manner of his death, we have the laconic note left by a local vicar, Richard Davies (vicar of Sapperton in Gloucestershire in the late seventeenth century), that "he died a papist". That is all; but that is a precious clue to the understanding of the deep meaning in the life and works of William Shakespeare.

Appendix – "The Papist and His Poet": The Jesuit Background to Shakespeare's Plays

In his *History of Great Britain*, published in 1611, John Speed makes an intriguing mention of "the papist and his poet". The papist in question is the prolific Jesuit pamphleteer, Robert Persons, who had recently published his account *Of Three Conversions of England* in 1603-4, including a detailed critique of John Foxe's *Book of Martyrs*. One of the earliest of Foxe's martyrs was the Lollard leader Sir John Oldcastle, who had suffered in the reign of Henry V and who came to be acclaimed by the Protestants as "morning star of the Reformation". In his critique Persons dismisses Oldcastle as "a ruffian knight, as all England knoweth, and commonly brought in by comedians on their stages". One of these unnamed comedians, if not the only one, is William Shakespeare, whose "ruffian knight" is better known to all England both then and since under his alias of Sir John Falstaff, whom Prince Hal addresses as "that father ruffian, that vanity in years" (*Henry IV Part I*, ii.4). His original name of Oldcastle is to be found not only in the probable source-play, *The Famous Victories of Henry the Fifth*, but also in Shakespeare's first Falstaff play, *Henry IV Part I*, where the Prince hails his boon companion as "my old lad of the castle" (i.2).

All this is common knowledge to Shakespeare scholars and requires no further elaboration here. But what calls for more precise consideration is the fact that this passing mention of "the papist and his poet", namely the Jesuit Persons and the dramatist Shakespeare, whom Speed dismissed (without naming them) as "of like conscience for lies, the one ever feigning and the other ever falsifying the truth", is unique in the writings of the age. The implied connection between them is, it is true, merely a literary or rather a gossipy one, not a personal relationship. In his book Persons merely speaks of Oldcastle as having been presented by unnamed comedians (in the plural) on the stage, with no further specification. Nor does Speed in his protest against Persons imply any closer form of relationship between "the papist and his poet", though the phrase is suggestive. And so most scholars are content to leave it at that, unique perhaps but nothing more.

But now, I wish to ask, is it really nothing more? In this passing mention may there not lurk a deeper connection in which, as Milton says in his *Il Penseroso*, "more is meant than meets the ear"? To explore this connection a beginning may be made by recalling the commonly known facts on either side, that of "the papist" (or Jesuit) and that of "his poet" (or dramatist). The facts are well known to both Elizabethan historians and Shakespeare scholars, but for some reason they are not commonly seen together, and so the interesting implications are rarely drawn.

On the one hand, it was in the summer of 1580 that the Jesuit Robert Persons arrived in England with his fellow Jesuit Edmund Campion and others, in what has been described with comic exaggeration as "the Jesuit invasion of England". By the December of the following year Campion had been executed as a "traitor" and Persons had retired to France; and so, it seemed, the "Jesuit invasion" was at an end. But the controversy to which their coming had given rise was by no means at an end. Both while the two Jesuits were still at large in England and after their disappearance from the English scene, there appeared during the first five years of that decade no fewer than eighty controversial books and pamphlets directly related to that coming. Some were admittedly of a more ephemeral nature, touching on almost every aspect of Campion's arrival in England, his activities throughout the country, his arrest and imprisonment in the Tower, his conferences in the Tower, his repeated tortures, his trial at Westminster Hall and his execution at Tyburn. Others raised questions of a more permanent and universal character, such as the English government's official use of torture on Catholic priests and laity and the imputation of an anti-Catholic "persecution" in England analogous to that conducted against the early Christian Church under the Roman Empire. Eventually, no less a personage than the Queen's chief adviser, Lord Burghley, felt obliged to defend the policy of his government with a shorter pamphlet and a longer book. The first was a brief *Declaration* of six pages, published in 1583, to refute the allegations of torture and to justify "the favourable dealing" and even the "clemency" of her majesty's government towards the late "traitors", who (he claimed) had been justly punished for their proven crimes of treason. The second was a larger and more general defence, published in the same year, of *The Execution of Justice in England*. The importance attached by the eminent author especially to the second of these writings may be gauged by its publication not only in English but also in French and Latin, written as it was to convince not only the English subjects of Queen Elizabeth but also readers of learning and influence overseas.

This particular controversy had only recently died down by the time Shakespeare is presumed to have arrived in London and to have begun his career on the stage there, towards the end of the 1580s; and its echoes still reverberated in the ears of Londoners, especially those with "papist" sympathies. Yet the Jesuits had by no means despaired of what they regarded as "the English mission". Campion had died a martyr's death, and Persons had withdrawn to the continent; but there were other English Jesuits who followed in their footsteps, mindful of Tertullian's ancient dictum that "the blood of martyrs is the seed of the Church". If Persons had seemed to run away from the dust of conflict, it was the more effectively to direct the activities of other Jesuits working in England, besides providing them with the writings they needed in their labours. By far the most successful of these writings was his popular "Book of Resolution", which was first published in 1582 as *The First Book of the Christian Exercise* and later, from 1585 onwards, retitled *The Christian Directory*. In 1584 it was reprinted under English Protestant auspices and as such became an instant best-seller, thus coming into the hands of Protestant no less than Catholic readers. One of its readers, to judge from its many echoes in his subsequent plays, was apparently William Shakespeare. More controversial, however, was a book that came out in the following decade under the title *A Conference about the Next Succession*, popularly known as

"The Book of Succession" and commonly attributed to Persons, though he himself never admitted any part in the publication. It never became a best-seller like the previous "Book of Resolution", but it was far more notorious at the time, while continuing to exercise an important influence on the development of English politics throughout the seventeenth century.

The further history of the Jesuit background to Shakespeare's plays was by no means confined to these and other writings of Persons. Rather, from the time of Campion onwards, as if in fulfilment of his famous brag, "For know, we have made a league . . .", other English Jesuits came, in wave upon wave, back to their native country for all the difficulties and dangers they knew awaited them. After the martyrdom of Campion and his companions (one of whom, Thomas Cottam, was the brother of one of Shakespeare's probable schoolmasters at Stratford), the superior of the few Jesuits in England was Jasper Heywood, an uncle of the poet John Donne and one of the English translators of the Latin tragedies of Seneca. When he was deported to France in 1585, his place was taken by William Weston, who soon became notorious for his part in certain exorcisms carried out in the late 1580s at a Catholic house near London, and in the so-called "Wisbech stirs" that led to a virulent controversy between some of the seminary priests who had been confined in Wisbech Castle and the Jesuits, notably Persons. When Weston was committed to Wisbech in 1587, his place as superior was taken over by Henry Garnet, who had come to England the previous year in company with the poet and future martyr Robert Southwell.

The latter soon made his name as a writer both of devotional poetry and of a euphuistic style of prose applied to religious themes. It was, strangely enough, in the very year of his death, 1595, that the bulk of his poetry was published in two volumes, *Saint Peter's Complaint* and *Maeoniae*, with the approval of the Archbishop of Canterbury. As Christopher Devlin has amply shown in his *Life of Robert Southwell*, these poems exercised no less deep an influence on the minds of literary contemporaries than Persons' "Book of Resolution". He even detects a pattern of religious conversion (not necessarily to Catholicism) in contemporary writings of the mid-1590s (even including Shakespeare's *Rape of Lucrece*) and attributes it to the combined influence of these two Jesuit writers.

As for Henry Garnet, he was more skilful in eluding the vigilance of the government spies and pursuivants. After guiding the affairs of the English Jesuits for almost twenty years with remarkable prudence, he was projected against his will into the limelight of public attention for his forced connection with the Gunpowder Plot of 1605. In the following year he was put on trial at Westminster Hall and sentenced to a traitor's death at Tyburn, thus following in the footsteps of Campion and Southwell, as well as many other English Jesuits and seminary priests. Only, because of the political circumstances of his trial and execution, he has been denied the posthumous honours of beatification and canonization accorded to those others. Another point of fame that Garnet came to share with Southwell in his trial was the issue of equivocation, a word that chiefly came into the English language (in its moral sense) on the former occasion and became even more notorious on the latter occasion.

2.

The foregoing is but a summary of the activities and writings of certain prominent Jesuits associated with "the English mission" from the time of their first arrival in 1580 till the death of their leader and champion, Robert Persons, in 1610. It may serve to show how closely it all coincides with the dramatic career of William Shakespeare, which roughly spans the two decades from 1590 to 1610, that is, from his first production of such early plays as *Titus Andronicus* and the three parts of *Henry VI* (though no one can say precisely which of his plays is the earliest) to his last production of *The Tempest* (to omit such plays as *Henry VIII* and *Two Noble Kinsmen* in which there are evident signs of collaboration with another, younger dramatist). In view of this coincidence, one may pass from "the one hand" of the Jesuit writings and activities to "the other hand" of Shakespeare's plays, beginning with the natural (though all too often unasked) question as to how far the dramatist was aware of those writings and activities, and also how far he may have been influenced by them. Not that Shakespeare scholars have hitherto turned a blind eye to those writings and activities; but for the most part they deal with them piecemeal, insofar as one or other action or publication had an ascertainable impact on a particular play.

Thus in the above-mentioned case of the characterization of Sir John Falstaff, it is not the poet-dramatist who is responding to the book of the papist-Jesuit; but it is a unique case of a contemporary Jesuit glancing at a play by the dramatist, if only in general, plural terms. No other Jesuit of the time so much as mentions Shakespeare or any of his plays by name, any more than Shakespeare mentions any of them or even their Society by name – though he seems to come close to doing so in the Porter scene of *Macbeth* (ii.3). It is as if between "the papist and his poet" there is a mutual conspiracy of silence.

All the same, on looking more closely into the plays of Shakespeare one by one, it is surprising how many of them contain passages in which scholars have detected allusions to Jesuit activities or writings, with varying degrees of certainty, probability and possibility. To go back to the early *Comedy of Errors*, the scene depicting the exorcism of Antipholus of Ephesus by the schoolmaster Pinch (iv.4) is traced with considerable probability to the exorcisms practised in the late 1580s (as mentioned above) by William Weston and a number of seminary priests (including Shakespeare's fellow-Stratfordian, Robert Debdale). Only, Shakespeare seems to elude this identification by borrowing the odd name of Pinch from the contemporary author of a book criticizing the exorcisms from a Protestant viewpoint, one R. Phinch (not otherwise known), whose *Knowledge and Appearance of the Church* (1590) comes conveniently in between the exorcisms and the presumed date for the *Comedy of Errors* in the early 1590s.

The first play in which Persons makes an alleged appearance is the other early comedy of

Love's Labour's Lost. This is a play which, more than almost any other of Shakespeare's, is riddled with contemporary allusion and innuendo, and on which much scholarly ingenuity has been expended without reaching any certain or at least generally accepted identification. Among other passages in which contemporary allusions have been recognized are two exchanges of wit (in the same scene, iv.2) between the pedant Holofernes and the parson Sir Nathaniel. On Jaquenetta's conventional greeting of the parson, "God give you good morrow, master parson", the pedant comments with the laboured pun, "Master parson, quasi pers-on; and if one should be pierced, which is the one?" Subsequently, when the parson refers to the saying of "a certain Father", the pedant checks him saying, "Sir, tell me not of the Father; I do fear colourable colours" – or specious pretexts (for treason). This is all explained with reference to Father Persons and his recently published "Book of Succession"; though another sufficient explanation is found in the other contemporary book by Gabriel Harvey, *Pierce's Supererogation* (1593), written in reply to Thomas Nash's *Pierce Penniless* (1592). These two books are central to the famous "flyting" between these two authors which forms no small part of the esoteric background of Shakespeare's play, in which the pedant is frequently identified with Harvey and the witty page Moth with Nash. Of course, it is not unlikely, given the notorious fondness of the dramatist for punning and topical allusion, that references to both books, by Persons and Harvey, were intended.

As for Robert Southwell, Christopher Devlin in his above-mentioned *Life of Robert Southwell* makes much of the possibility that the dedication of his first book of poems, *Saint Peter's Complaint*, "To my worthy good cousin, Master W.S.", is not so much to his lawyer cousin William Shelley as to his literary cousin (as well as distant cousin by marriage) William Shakespeare. At least, Southwell is evidently making both a complaint about the many contemporary poets who devote their wit to "Venus' rose" (with seeming reference to Shakespeare's recent *Venus and Adonis*, published in 1593) and an appeal to such poets to show rather "how well verse and virtue suit together" (with seeming anticipation of Shakespeare's *The Rape of Lucrece*, published in the following year). This is all, no doubt, on the mere level of probability, though a fascinating one, as Devlin pursues his line of argument in a whole chapter entitled "Master W.S." More important, however, are the many phrases in *Saint Peter's Complaint*, not to mention other poems by Southwell, that seem to have been taken up by the dramatist and echoed especially in his four "great" tragedies. The same may be said of the literary impact of Persons' "Book of Resolution" on Shakespeare's plays, not least on those four "great" tragedies.

Then there is the above-mentioned discussion on the morality of "equivocation" that emerged at Southwell's trial in 1595 and developed into a full-scale controversy, in which Persons also took a leading part, after Garnet's trial in 1606. It may have been (as commentators explain) with the former trial in mind that Hamlet protests against the inveterate punning of the clown in the graveyard scene (v.l): "How absolute the knave is! We must speak by the card, or equivocation will undo us". Here, however, "equivocation" is a mere punning or quibbling on words, with no implication of the moral problem discussed by Southwell at his trial, with reference to the contemporary teaching of Jesuit moralists abroad. On the other hand, the subsequent allusion to "an equivocator ... who committed treason enough for God's sake, yet could not equivocate to heaven", in the Porter scene in *Macbeth* (ii.3), points more clearly to the other trial of Garnet; and this identification is seen as confirmed by the other mention of a "farmer" coming to the same gate of hell, considering that "Farmer" was also an alias of Garnet. So it has become a commonplace of Shakespeare scholarship not only to identify the equivocator and the farmer with Garnet but also to assign the date of *Macbeth* to the summer of 1606, after both the trial and the prompt publication of its proceedings in *A True and Perfect Relation*, whose wording seems to be echoed in several psssages of the play.

Lastly, it may be asked, what of Campion, whose arrest, tortures, trial and execution in 1581 did so much to initiate and inspire the subsequent Jesuit activities and writings in England, not least during the very time of Shakespeare's career on the London stage? Allusion has been detected, if not to Campion by name, at least to the similar cases of Robert Southwell, Henry Walpole and John Cornelius, in the concluding and cryptic couplet of Sonnet 124: "To this I witness call the fools of time,/ Which die for goodness, who have lived for crime." Here, however, it is difficult to say anything with probability, let alone certainty, about the identification of these words, save that the

Catholic martyrs of the age, whether Jesuit or otherwise, who were invariably sentenced on the charge of "treason", would fit the description reasonably well. It may be added that Jesuits are expected, according to their Rule, to become (if need be) fools for the sake of Christ; and in the context of the sonnet they are expected to bear witness to the "hugely politic" stance of love, transcending the variations of time. Secondly, a reminiscence of Campion's speech of self-defence at his trial has been detected in Hermione's similar speech in *The Winter's Tale* (iii.2). But this is no more than an interesting parallel, without any convincing verbal echoes from the Jesuit martyr to the dramatic heroine.

Only in *King Lear* the experience not only of Campion, but also of Weston, Southwell, Garnet and almost all the Jesuit priests engaged on "the English mission", may be seen to have its exact parallel in the pitiful condition of Edgar. The way he is obliged to leave his father's house, to put on disguise and change his name, to elude the "guard and most unusual vigilance" set up against him, including the "intelligence" given by spies and informers, in accordance with official "proclamations", and so to "lurk" in corners and even to pretend possession by an evil spirit (ii.3, iii.6) – all this is matched point by point with the experience of both the Jesuits and the seminary priests on the English mission. As Campion himself said from the outset in a letter to the Jesuit General in 1580: "I cannot long escape the hands of the heretics; the enemy have so many eyes, so many tongues, so many scouts and crafts. I am in apparel to myself very ridiculous; I often change my name also ...

Threatening edicts come forth against us daily." Such were the proclamations that came forth about this time, one dated July 15, soon after the arrival of the Jesuits in England, and another dated January 10, 1581, "against the retaining of Jesuits". This was but the beginning of a long process of anti-Catholic and specifically anti-Jesuit repression, that was periodically stepped up at the prompting of Puritan members of Parliament, till Robert Southwell could justly complain in his *Humble Supplication to Her Majesty* (not published till 1600): "We are made the common theme of every railing declaimer, abused without hope or means of remedy, by every wretch with most infamous names; no tongue so forsworn but it is of credit against us, none so true but it is thought false in our defence." Above all, Edgar's resort to a pretence of diabolic possession is literally derived from Samuel Harsnett's anti-Papist *Declaration of Egregious Popish Impostures*, which, though not published till 1604 (only a year or so before Shakespeare presumably began the composition of *King Lear*), is directed against the exorcisms carried out by Weston and Debdale in the late 1580s, owing to the recent discovery of a manuscript "Book of Miracles" describing those events from the Catholic point of view.

3.

All these allusions, most of which are admitted by the majority of Shakespeare scholars, serve no doubt to bring the plays of Shakespeare closer to their Papist and Jesuit background. But in the outcome, they seem to constitute a rejection of that background, such as one also finds more explicitly in the contemporary life and writings of John Donne. When we take these allusions on their face value, we find Persons ridiculed as a traitor, with his "colourable colours", and his fellow-Jesuits as "fools of time", who, whatever goodness may have appeared in their endurance of death for the sake of religion, have "lived for crime". Then, both Southwell and Garnet (especially the latter) are seemingly scorned as "equivocators", who may quibble before men on earth but can hardly get away with their quibbling before the judgment seat of God. As for the exorcisms practised by Weston, they seem to be parodied in the case of Pinch and even depicted as diabolic in the case of Edgar. The fact that Edgar's language is so liberally borrowed from Harsnett is interpreted as a sign that the dramatist shared his viewpoint; and an anti-Jesuit significance has even been detected in the name of Edgar's persecuting brother Edmund, as echoing both the Christian name of Campion and the alias of Weston, Edmonds.

Such is perhaps what may be read, or heard, on the surface of the plays, or else between their lines, according to the bias of the interpreter. Yet Shakespeare himself not infrequently warns his readers, or listeners, against the danger of being deceived by outward appearances. "So may the outward forms be least themselves," comments Bassanio before making his choice among the three caskets in *The Merchant of Venice*, "the world is still deceiv'd with ornament"; and he goes on in the same speech to mention "the seeming truth that cunning times put on to entrap the wisest" (iii.2). Indeed, the more familiar one becomes with the Jesuit background of Shakespeare's plays, the more one realizes how carefully the priests had to proceed in order to elude the continual vigilance of spies and informers, as Campion emphasized in his above-quoted letter. One also comes upon case after case of the cunning propaganda orchestrated by the English government against them, not only in writings like *The Execution of Justice* by Lord Burghley himself, but also in the many anti-Jesuit pamphlets written by Puritans at the instigation or at least with the encouragement of Burghley.

As for the occasional jests at the crime of "treason" committed by the Jesuits and seminary priests and their resort to the subterfuge of equivocation, they may well be dismissed as gimmicks for groundlings, to elicit an easy laugh from a Protestant audience and perhaps to distract their attention from the more serious meaning of the dramatist. After all, in such an age which, as Portia complains in the above-quoted scene from *The Merchant of Venice* (iii.2), "puts bars between the owners and their rights", the dramatist may not have wished his serious meaning (from a secretly Catholic viewpoint) to be readily apparent to a largely Protestant audience. In this respect, he may be compared (as in other respects, too) to the Duke in *Measure for Measure*, whose "givings out" are described as being "of an infinite distance from his true meant design" (i.4).

To take the case of equivocation, for example. Hamlet may wrily complain of its too liberal use by the grave-digger (though such quibbling is criticized as "the fatal Cleopatra" of Shakespeare himself); and the Porter in *Macbeth* may imagine one condemned not only to death but even to hell for his reliance on equivocation. Yet in at least two of his plays the dramatist implies his sympathy with a less subtle form of equivocation, or the downright telling of a lie, as a means of bringing about the necessary happy ending of a comedy. Thus, to return to the Duke in *Measure for Measure*, who is strangely reminiscent of the English Jesuits – partly for his adoption of a friar's habit (both Persons and Garnet were given the name of "friar" by their enemies), partly for his ministry to "the afflicted spirits" in prison (ii.3), partly for his reputation of lurking in "dark corners" (iv.3): he justifies his plan to deceive Angelo with a "bed-trick", in a strange incantatory tone of voice, "So disguise shall, by the disguis'd,/ Pay with falsehood false exacting" (iii.2). In the same way, Helena, the heroine of the parallel problem comedy of *All's Well That Ends Well*, justifies a similar use of the "bed-trick" on her false husband Bertram, in a similarly incantatory tone of voice, "Only in this disguise I think't no sin/ To cozen him that would unjustly win" (iv.2). In both cases, it may be remarked, Shakespeare not only implicitly justifies the Jesuit use of equivocation but he even betters their instruction, without resort to the casuistical justification of seeming deceit which the Jesuit moralists (including Garnet and Persons) felt it necessary to make for protecting the Augustinian principle that a lie is always immoral and sinful, if sometimes but venially so.

But to return to *The Merchant of Venice*, what (it may be asked) might have been the serious meaning of the dramatist, from which he would have wanted to distract the attention of a largely Protestant audience? Isn't it a contradiction for the dramatist to have put a serious meaning into his play without wanting his audience to notice it? At least one such meaning he might well have had in mind, given both the known religious situation in contemporary England (when the Catholics were at the height of their sufferings, with no remedy in sight) and the probable recusant connections of the dramatist (looking back to both his parents and forwards to his daughter Susanna), would have been a Catholic meaning. After all, the main theme of the play is centred on Portia's moving plea for mercy against the rigid legal justice which Shylock claims as his right. Within the setting of the play in Venice, which may easily be seen in terms of Elizabethan London, the poor victim Antonio is described as "one in whom the ancient Roman honour more appears", where "Roman" may easily be interpreted no less as Roman Catholic than as "classical Roman". On the other hand, the villain Shylock, with all his Jewishness, shows not a few traits of those Puritans who were the most zealous persecutors of the Catholics – as some eminent Shakespeare scholars have pointed out. Thus one may say that, with the contemporary religious situation in mind, Shakespeare is aiming, at least indirectly and in general terms, at eliciting the sympathy and human feelings of his audience, though without pointing too clearly at the victims he has in mind, owing to the danger to himself and his mission as a dramatist.

4.

Such an interpretation of *The Merchant of Venice* has, I confess, been put forward (so far as I know) by no other Shakespeare scholar. So it may well evoke both astonishment and disbelief, such as are often accorded to a new theory that runs counter to existing notions. Yet all I ask for at this stage is that it be at least considered as a working hypothesis, according to the custom of scientific theory. Isn't it, to begin with, at least possible in the historical background of Shakespeare's England? Doesn't it fit in with what we know about Shakespeare's life and plays, setting aside (for the time being) other interpretations? Or rather, doesn't it fit in with this knowledge better than any other theory? And doesn't it go far towards explaining the enigma which all students of Shakespeare feel about him, and which is hardly otherwise explicable? After all, for a new theory to be accepted about Shakespeare's life and plays, it has to do more than fit the facts as well as any other theory: it has to fit them better, in order to replace the others. Not that there are many theories that profess to explain the Shakespearian enigma. For the most part, scholars seem content to leave it as an enigma, like Stonehenge, and to devote their attention to the particular meanings of particular plays. On a more general level, it is commonly doubted whether Shakespeare had any "deeper" meaning in his plays; and George Bernard Shaw even criticized him for his lack of any serious philosophy or viewpoint of his own.

This new theory has, moreover, to encounter the reluctance of many Shakespeare scholars not only to explain an enigma, which is for them as inexplicable as the phenomenon of genius, but also to admit any allegorical meaning in the plays. Nowadays, the very suggestion of such a meaning is dismissed as a form of "allegorizing", if not "theologizing", and attributed to an unwillingness to accept the natural, realistic interpretation of the plays. Such criticism, however, may in turn be attributed to an unwillingness to recognize any hidden or allegorical meaning in the plays, even though it may be there. The basic question is rather how the plays are to be read and understood: whether in a modern context, within which readers have come to inherit a long tradition of realistic interpretation, dating back to the late seventeenth century, or in the contemporary terms of post-mediaeval, Elizabethan drama. Today there seems to be a widespread prejudice among scholars against allegorization, or what is regarded as the reading of allegories into Shakespeare's plays – assuming what has to be proved, that there are no such allegories in the plays. It has also been pointed out that Shakespeare himself, through the character of Fluellen in *Henry V*, ridicules the temptation to find "figures in all things" (iv.7) – as though anticipating the later tendency of certain scholars. But this episode may also be interpreted as an instance of humour at the dramatist's own expense, analogous to Theseus' criticism of "the poet" in the last scene of *A Midsummer Night's Dream*, as "of imagination all compact", like the lunatic and the lover.

Anyhow, from the high Middle Ages right into the Renaissance the tide of allegorical interpretation was, like "the sea of faith", "at the full" – as may be seen fully exemplified in two such notable poets as Shakespeare's great Italian predecessor Dante and his fellow-countryman Spenser. Not only are their representative poems, the *Divina Commedia* and the *Faerie Queene*, susceptible of an allegorical interpretation, but the poets themselves draw explicit attention to their allegorical intentions in their letters, that of Dante to Can Grande and that of Spenser to Sir Walter Raleigh. This is no matter for surprise, seeing how deeply the allegorical mentality had entered into the mediaeval world-view from the time of Origen and Augustine and indeed of Paul himself; and such was the world-view inherited by Shakespeare – a world-view that only came to be discarded with the rise of Puritanism and science in the seventeenth century, both of which were for different reasons opposed to allegory. There is, however, a significant difference to be noted between Spenser's use of allegory and that which I am proposing for Shakespeare. The former is more openly moral, and less mythical, in the explanation he gives about his use of allegory in the *Faerie Queene* in his letter to Raleigh; and to that extent he is also different from the more mediaeval poet of the *Divina Commedia*. But what I am now proposing in the plays of Shakespeare is a more personal or historical allegory, as when he takes the events of mediaeval English history in his series of history plays and interprets them in the light of more recent events in his own time. Of special interest in this connection is the glimpse afforded by a distinguished contemporary witness into the topical meaning of *Richard II*, when the play was revived in early 1601 on the eve of the Essex rebellion. This was no less a person than Queen Elizabeth, who is said to have remarked indignantly to the antiquarian William Lambarde (a remark that he himself recorded), *à propos* of the deposition scene (iv.1), "I am Richard II, know ye not that?" If she saw herself in Richard, one is led to wonder in how many other characters of Shakespeare's plays she might not have recognized herself – as she has been variously recognized by later scholars in King John, in Claudius and Gertrude, in Lady Macbeth and in Cleopatra.

5.

Now, to return to *The Merchant of Venice* and its possible interpretation in the light of contemporary recusant history, one may also recall the odd, riddling exchange of wit between Portia and Bassanio just before the latter enters upon his choice among the three caskets. It is one of the most protracted among the many passages to be gleaned from Shakespeare's plays that have a special (though not altogether unique) bearing on the plight of the papist recusants. It is precisely after Portia has complained of "these naughty times" that "put bars between the owners and their rights", that Bassanio insists on making his choice without further delay, since, "as I am, I live upon the rack" – with apparent reference to the kind of torture most commonly used on Catholic priests from the time of Campion onwards, for the purpose of extracting both a confession of treason and information about other priests and places of shelter. Then Portia takes him up on this image, adding, "Upon the rack, Bassanio! Then confess what treason there is mingled with your love." He replies, "None but that ugly treason of mistrust." Again Portia insists, as though to test the mind of Bassanio, and in strange anticipation of Malcolm's later testing of Macduff in *Macbeth* (iv.3), "Ay, but I fear you speak upon the rack, where men enforced do speak anything."

Such were the tortures, only too frequently used on Catholic prisoners in the Tower, which had to be justified by the above-mentioned writings of Lord Burghley against the rising tide of criticism in Catholic Europe. So far from being diminished in frequency or intensity by this criticism, they were rather increased, particularly under the personal supervision of Richard Topcliffe at his own houses and used with excruciating virulence on Robert Southwell in 1595 only a year or so before Shakespeare turned to the composition of this play. In such a context, the subsequent words of Bassanio assume an even more significant contemporary application, when he goes on to point his accusing finger at "the seeming truth which cunning times put on to entrap the wisest" (such seeming truth as Burghley urges in his arguments for *The Execution of Justice in England*), and when he therefore chooses the "plainness" of lead (taken as a symbol of recusancy) as moving him "more than eloquence".

This topical-allegorical interpretation of *The Merchant of Venice*, moreover, takes on further credibility when seen as applicable not just to this one play but to many others (if not all) of Shakespeare's plays as well. After all, the contemporary situation of English Catholic recusants hardly changed at all substantially during the twenty years of Shakespeare's stage career – except to become increasingly intolerable from year to year, till the climax was reached with the "discovery" of the Gunpowder Plot and its bitter aftermath. Then, as even the unfriendly prosecutor at

Garnet's trial, Sir Edward Coke, admitted, "If any one green leaf for Catholics could have been visibly discerned by the eye of (the conspirators), they would never have entered into practice with foreign princes." And Shakespeare himself, it may be added, is nothing if not topical, as in other respects admitted by all Shakespeare scholars, so surely and not least in this.

So from *The Merchant of Venice* one may well turn to the next major comedy of *As You Like It*, composed some two or three years later. From the outset of this play one comes upon a situation exactly parallel to that of the Catholic recusants, especially during the first decade of the reign of Queen Elizabeth. Here is a group of exiles gathered round the elder Duke in the Forest of Arden, in much the same way as in that first decade the Catholic exiles gathered in growing numbers round such leaders as Thomas Harding, Nicholas Sanders and above all William Allen – first at Louvain in the Low Countries and later at Douai in France, both places in the vicinity of the Ardennes. By contrast to the perils of "the envious court" (ii.1), here at least the exiles feel safe and even, as Celia insists, rejoicing in true "liberty" (i.3). Here, too, one finds not a few old religious men in the background, living in nooks "merely monastic" (iii.2), such as had long since been suppressed at home in England under the reign of Henry VIII – though there is mention in Shakespeare's youth of one such old religious man, a Marian priest, allowed to eke out his days at Temple Grafton in Shakespeare's Forest of Arden (in Warwickshire).

There is indeed a nostalgia for the "good old days" of merry England – or what the poet calls in

Sonnet 77, "days long since, before these last so bad" – running throughout the play. It is voiced particularly by Orlando, in speaking to his old servant Adam and commending him not only as a "good old man", but also as representing "the constant service of the antique world, when service sweat for duty, not for meed" (ii.3). He is, moreover, speaking in response to Adam's previous exclamation, "Your virtues, gentle master, are sanctified and holy traitors to you. O what a world is this, when what is comely envenoms him that bears it!" He also goes on to tell Adam, in the same vein, "Thou art not for the fashion of these times" – as it were echoing Portia's previous complaint of "these naughty times" (iii.2). Such is the world ruled over by the usurping Duke Frederick, who reveals his true self in banishing his niece Rosalind and rejecting her indignant protests of innocence. His words to her on that occasion, "Thus do all traitors. If their purgation did consist in words, they are as innocent as grace itself" (i.3), recall the similar assertion made by Lord Burghley in *The Execution of Justice in England*: "It hath been in all ages and in all countries a common usage for all offenders for the most part, both great and small, to make defence of their lewd and unlawful facts by untruths and by colouring and covering their deeds (were they never so vile) with pretences of some other causes."

Such indeed, at least for the Catholic recusants, much more than for the Puritans, was the reign of Queen Elizabeth in England. For all their professions of loyalty to the Queen and her government at least in matters temporal, they were treated and severely punished as traitors according to the full rigour of the law. As Southwell also complains in his *Humble Supplication*, "So heavy is the hand of our superiors against us, that we generally are accounted men whom it is a credit to pursue, a disgrace to protect, a commodity to spoil, a gain to torture, and a glory to kill."

6.

These two notable comedies, belonging to the period of 1596-99, stand out from the others both for their more serious content, which is hardly less tragic than comic, and for their corresponding applicability to the contemporary recusant situation. Thus they serve to anticipate the plays of Shakespeare's "tragic period" from *Hamlet* onwards. This tragedy, which is better described as a "problem play", stands (in 1601-2) at the turning-point of Shakespeare's stage career, as the sixteenth moves into the seventeenth century and the age of the Tudor Elizabeth is replaced (in 1603) by that of the Stuart James. In it and in the subsequent tragedies the recusant situation may be seen even more poignantly re-enacted in what I have called allegorical-topical terms.

From the beginning of the play Hamlet is presented, against an apparently Lutheran background, as fresh from his university studies at Wittenberg (a name that is significantly repeated four times in the second scene), with a brooding emphasis on the corruption of human nature as a result of original sin. "Man," he exclaims, "delights not me" (ii.2); and again, "We are arrant knaves, all; believe none of us" (iii.1). But it is not as a Lutheran that he finds himself at odds with the new political order of Denmark and in sympathy with the old order personified in "the majesty of buried Denmark", his own father (i.1). He is no Puritan, who also may be said to have disagreed with the new order of Queen Elizabeth, not so much because of the Queen herself (whom they regarded as basically on their side) as because of her failure to go far enough along the road to reform. Rather, if a typical Puritan is to be found in the play, it is Hamlet's rival, the fiery young Laertes who, for all his association with the Catholic (or Gallican) University of Paris, reveals his Puritanism in his rejection of tradition, "as the world were now but to begin, antiquity forgot, custom not known" (iv.5). His type may be seen in the Puritan Martin Marprelate (also parodied in Sir Oliver Martext, in *As You Like It* iii.3), who is described by Thomas Cooper in his contemporary *Admonition to the People of England* (1589) as "a flaming firebrand". (This description is further echoed by the Clown in *All's Well That Ends Well* i.3, where he names the Puritan "Charbon", or firecoal.)

As for the enigmatic character of Hamlet, so strangely similar in this and other respects to that of Shakespeare himself, his deeply felt need to hold his tongue though his heart should break (i.2) is precisely parallel to that felt by the Catholic recusants of the time, not by the Puritans who were ever ready to speak out. It is the Catholics who sympathized with that old order of England which had died with the death of Queen Mary, and who now found themselves out of sympathy with the new order that had come in with the accession of Queen Elizabeth. In her accession, it may be added, one who had been chiefly instrumental on her behalf was Sir William Cecil, later Lord Burghley, who has been compared to the Lord Polonius (a name that might be taken as a Latinized form, with a Welsh pronunciation, of Burghley), both for his sententious and officious wisdom and for his addiction to spying or (as it was then called) "intelligence".

Above all, the dilemma of Hamlet, as stated by him in the seemingly metaphysical terms of "To be, or not to be", and echoed by Shakespeare himself in the more personal terms of Sonnet 76, "Tir'd with all these, for restful death I cry", is exactly (in contemporary terms) parallel to that of the Catholic recusants in England. Many of them, not least the younger members of the recusant gentry, many of them Shakespeare's own relatives through his mother, Mary Arden, were facing the difficult choice of either living and enduring the constant persecution or doing something desperate to end the existing order, even though they should die in the attempt. The second alternative was, in fact, the choice made by those Catholic gentlemen who had attached themselves to the cause of Essex in his ill-fated rebellion of 1601, and who went on to become involved in the Gunpowder Plot (without realising they were only playing into the cunning hands of Sir Robert Cecil, who even then was accused as ringleader of this plot to ruin the Catholic cause in England). Hamlet, however, in his reluctance to make a definite choice, seems to incline rather to the first alternative, which (in contemporary terms) was that continually urged by the Jesuits and other priests in their various epistles of comfort and consolation to the afflicted Catholics, including one by Southwell himself. Thus, insofar as Shakespeare himself is to be seen in the character of Hamlet, he would appear in basic agreement with the Jesuit policy of prudence and endurance (as incarnated in Henry Garnet) – despite the exaggerated reputation of that Order for advocating the rash expedient of tyrannicide, owing to the scholastic theory put forth by one Jesuit, Juan de Mariana.

Between *Hamlet* and *Macbeth* there lies (according to the computation of most Shakespeare scholars) an interval of five years; but the two plays are closely connected – in subject-matter (the history of the early eleventh century on either side of the North Sea), in the abundant use of soliloquy by the hero, and in the way the hero of the latter play comes to choose (not without hesitation) the second of the alternatives considered by the hero of the former, "to take arms" though hardly "against a sea of troubles". The dramatic situation of the two heroes is, of course, different in detail. Macbeth is in no dilemma about whether to take the course of revenge or of suicide; though he does feel a dilemma about whether to do the deed of murder, to which he is prompted by his own ambition, the suggestion of the witches and the urging of his wife, or not. But the way the two heroes severally reflect the contemporary politico-religious situation is deeply significant. Hamlet's dilemma is, as mentioned above, remarkably similar to that of the recusant followers of the Earl of Essex in his rebellion of 1601; and Hamlet himself is even compared in his melancholy to the Earl. As for Macbeth's deed, it is even more obviously related to that of the Gunpowder plotters, some of whom (such as their leader Robert Catesby) had come to the Plot from the Rebellion. Even on the surface of the play, the Porter scene (ii.3), as has been mentioned, contains obvious reference to the very recent trial of Garnet, as well as to the published proceedings of the trial; and this provides scholars with a basic clue to the dating of the play's composition. And even granted the conjecture of Coleridge that the scene was a later addition, even from a pen other than Shakespeare's, there are enough echoes in the course of the play from the above-mentioned *True Relation of the Late Proceedings* to confirm the reference. Thus the emphasis of Sir Edward Coke on "the monstrousness and continual horror of this so desperate a cause ... without any name" seems to be echoed by Macduff on his return from the king's chamber, "O horror! horror! horror! Tongue nor heart cannot conceive nor name thee!" (ii.3)

On the other hand, it is necessary in dealing with this as with the previous plays to look beneath the surface – in which the dramatist seems to be adopting the official government position and condemning the Jesuit recourse to equivocation which he even seems to call in Macbeth's words, "the equivocation of the fiend" (v.5) – in order to touch the hidden, allegorical-topical meaning. This meaning may be traced in three stages. First, there are the other words of Macduff, following on his horrified exclamation, when he goes on to identify his horror not at any equivocation but at the way "confusion now hath made his masterpiece" and "most sacrilegious murder hath broke ope the Lord's anointed temple, and stole thence the life o' the building" (v.3). The conventional topical application of these words is to the design of the plotters to blow up the Houses of Parliament, with everyone in them; only, theirs was a deed that remained undone, as it was prevented by a timely "discovery". On the other hand, one may recall another deed of destruction that was not only done, less than seventy years before, but was also sacrilegious in the full sense of the word, breaking open as it did not one but many anointed temples of the Lord and thus creating many masterpieces of confusion. I mean the dissolution of the monasteries undertaken by Henry VIII from 1536 to 1540, leaving a sad trail of "bare ruin'd choirs" (as Shakespeare calls them in Sonnet 73) up and down the English countryside. It was directly as a result of this "masterpiece" of confusion and its subsequent ratification by Henry's daughter Elizabeth, that England came to be described by Catholic writers in exile in much the same terms as those used of Scotland by Lennox and Ross, Malcolm and Macduff, who join in a chorus of lamentation over "our suffering country" (iii.6) and "our poor country" (iv.3).

As for what Macbeth calls "the equivocation of the fiend that lies like truth" (v.5), insofar as it may be said to express the dramatist's indignation against the Gunpowder Plot, it may be viewed in the light of Bassanio's warning against "the seeming truth that cunning times put on to entrap the wisest" (iii.2). In other words, it is not so much the Jesuit Garnet or even the Catholic plotters who were guilty of this "equivocation of the fiend" – considering that the equivocation used by Garnet was (as the trial made sufficiently clear) never a means of destruction of others but merely of self-defence – as the English government under Sir Robert Cecil (recently created Earl of Salisbury) that had successfully "framed" these poor victims in the public eye. Even so, mutterings were heard even at the time, and even expressed in print, that the whole affair was Cecil's plot. Only, the dramatist could hardly point his finger in the play to what may well have been the true object of his indignation. All he could do was, like Lennox, to utter speeches that might hit the thoughts of some members of his audience which could "interpret further" (iii.6).

Finally, from *Hamlet* and *Macbeth* it is only natural to turn to Shakespeare's own masterpiece not so much of confusion as of reconciliation, *King Lear*. And this is also (to my mind) the play that comes closest to giving full expression to the dramatist's tragic reflections on the plight of the Catholic recusants in England. Here too, as in *As You Like It*, is a play on the theme of exile, in which the good characters are all sooner or later driven into exile by the bad. The first to go are Cordelia and Kent, followed shortly after by Edgar; and then her father Lear goes with his Fool, followed by Edgar's father Gloucester. Here, too, those in exile bear a marked resemblance not only to the English Catholics in exile in the Low Countries (as in Arden in *As You Like It*) but also to the hunted priests on returning to their native country. There "in disguise", as Edgar says of the faithful Kent, they may be said to have "follow'd (their) enemy king, and (done) him service improper for a slave" (v.3), where "king" may be interpreted as standing for his kingdom. As for the connection between Edgar's disguise as a madman and the exorcisms performed by Weston, Debdale and others, or rather the biased account of those exorcisms given by Samuel Harsnett, it has already been mentioned as belonging to the surface meaning of the play, or at least to the commonly accepted account of its contemporary sources. (Harsnett's book was published only a year or so before the composition of the play.) It has been interpreted as another casting of discredit on the Jesuits, insofar as the dramatist is regarded as in probable agreement with his source. But Edgar is no self-deluded maniac victimized by his brother Edmund, in the way Harsnett portrays the subjects of exorcism as victimized by the priests. Rather, in the circumstances of his escape from home and his choice of disguise, he is rather to be compared to the hunted priests, victimized by the English authorities and hounded by the spies, informers and pursuivants in their pay. Nor is it only the situation of Catholic recusants at home that is mirrored in the misery of the hunted Edgar. The plight of the Catholic exiles abroad is also seen in the rejection of Cordelia and her effective banishment to France, albeit as Queen of France. She is significantly accompanied to France by the loyal Kent, who in his subsequent return to Britain in disguise may also (as has been mentioned) be a reflection of the returning seminary priests and Jesuits. In this connection, there are two interesting points about the historical and topographical background of the play that are rarely noted or dwelt upon by commentators. One is the complete lack of any mention of "Britain" in the text of the play, but only as the "scene" in the table of *dramatis personae*, though the adjective "British" occurs three times, once in the mad ravings of Edgar (iii.4), and twice with reference to the British army under Albany and Edmund (iv.4,6). Yet Lear is King of Britain, no less than Cymbeline, in whose subsequent play the name of "Britain" recurs no less than twenty-seven times, and of "Briton" another eighteen times, with "British" only twice! One may conjecture that for the purpose of this play the dramatist wishes to avoid too close a connection of Lear with prehistoric Britain, so as to allow more possibility for his association with contemporary England (as the country was still officially called).

This association is further fostered by the other point, namely, the identification of the neighbouring kingdom on the other side of the narrow seas as France, not Gaul – though the name of France only came into being, like that of Burgundy, well over a millennium after the events supposedly happening in Lear's Britain. Thus, too, the dramatist may be seen as reinforcing the contemporary reference of the play. Above all, this reference culminates in the manner of Cordelia's return, both when she insists on her arrival with the French army in Dover, "No blown ambition doth our arms incite,/ But love, dear love, and our ag'd father's right" (iv.4), and when she laments after their arrest by the British under Edmund, "We are not the first/ Who with best meaning have incurr'd the worst" (v.3). In both her statements one may notice an incantatory tone of voice not unlike that of the Duke in *Measure for Measure* or that of Helena in *All's Well That Ends Well*. Such was no doubt the insistence, and the lamentation, on the occasion of the sailing and the defeat of the Spanish Armada of 1588, if not of the King of Spain himself (about whose purity of intention there may be room for doubt), at least of the English Catholic exiles under the leadership of Cardinal Allen and Father Robert Persons, who both lent their full support to the enterprise.

In conclusion, after the foregoing consideration of two major comedies and three of the "four
great tragedies", there remain certain general objec-
tions against the "recusant" hypothesis to be dealt
with. One such objection is the seeming lack of any
contemporary recognition, even on the Catholic or
more specifically the Jesuit side, of this hidden layer
of "recusant" meaning in the plays. Even John
Speed, who speaks somewhat contemptuously of
"this papist and his poet", restricts his reference to
the Falstaff plays, without any indication that the
poet in question may also be a papist. Even on the
Jesuit side, though in another country (Spain) and
in another age (some decades later), the first explicit
connection between the Society of Jesus and the
plays of Shakespeare takes the odd form of the first
"bowdlerization" of the plays by an English Jesuit at
the college of Valladolid, including the entire deletion of what has been called Shakespeare's "most
Catholic play", *Measure for Measure*, and the omission of the anti-papal speeches in *King John* (iii.1).
This is seen as a proof of the dramatist's unfavour-
able reception by the recusants; though the rough
attempts at censorship might be construed in an
opposite sense, as showing the censor's desire to put
Shakespeare's plays into the hands of his recusant
pupils at the college. The entire deletion of *Measure for Measure*, for all its Catholic content, may be
sufficiently explained by reason of its "adult" nature
in the treating of "fornication".

As for the comparative absence of any
contemporary notice of the plays and their hidden

meaning on the recusant side, this may be explained by the presumed desire of the dramatist to remain in disguise till the very end. Such is the example he gives in *King Lear* of both Kent and Edgar: where Kent insists, in spite of Cordelia's contrary urging, "Yet to be known shortens my made intent" (iv.7), and Edgar lives to regret his own insistence on not having revealed himself to his father earlier and to exclaim against it as a "fault" (v.3). Only indirectly, and as it were at a remove from the dramatist's "givings out", is there some contemporary indication of the way the wind is blowing from *King Lear* onwards. First, there is the simple mention of the name of Shakespeare's favourite daughter Susanna on the recusancy returns for 1606, when a special search was being made for Catholic recusants in the aftermath of the Gunpowder Plot; and thus she may be seen as following in the footsteps of her grandfather John Shakespeare, whose name had similarly appeared on the recusancy returns for 1592. Secondly, there is the more serious case of the conviction of a Catholic recusant gentleman in Yorkshire for entertaining a group of players at his own and other recusant houses, where they had been presenting in 1609-10 certain anti-Protestant plays, besides Shakespeare's *King Lear* and *Pericles*, which had both recently been printed in quarto. This latter evidence, which has only come to light in the past few years, affords some sign of contemporary recusant appreciation of at least these two plays. It is not just that they happened to be readily available in quarto form, to provide some cover to the more obviously anti-Protestant plays; but these two plays together, when seen in the light of their hidden meaning, would have offered a deep consolation to the recusants during the fearful aftermath of the Gunpowder Plot. At the same time, the strange concluding words of Edgar or Albany, spoken again in an incantatory tone of voice, "The oldest hath borne most: we that are young/ Shall never see so much nor live so long" (v.3), would surely have reverberated with a special meaning in the ears and minds of the recusant audience.

Further, in the light of all that has been said about this layer of hidden reference to the recusants in the plays, one may more readily receive the old gossip concerning Shakespeare's end retailed by a Gloucestershire clergyman towards the end of the seventeenth century, that "he died a papist". Thus not only his father John and his daughter Susanna, but William Shakespeare himself is seen, at least in death, in the ranks of the recusants; and this recusancy of his may further be seen as supporting the foregoing evidence of a recusant meaning in the plays. On the other hand, this gossip is rejected out of hand by Shakespeare's latest authoritative biographer, on the grounds that it is mere gossip, and not borne out by any hard evidence in the plays themselves. But it all depends on how one interprets the evidence of the plays, whether on their face value, as the Protestant members of the audience were no doubt meant to understand them, or in view of a hidden meaning such as would be apparent to recusant members of the audience, like those who came to the performances of *King Lear* and *Pericles* at the above-mentioned recusant houses in Yorkshire.

Still, it may be insisted, considering (as Shakespeare says in *The Merchant of Venice* ii.2, if through the mouth of a clown) that "truth will come to light", why has the truth of a hidden recusant meaning (if it is the truth) remained concealed so long from "the yet unknowing world" (*Hamlet* v.2)? From the late Victorian age onwards there has not been wanting a succession of Shakespeare scholars to claim the hidden recusancy of William Shakespeare as a matter of biography. Only, they have hardly entered into the deeper meaning of the plays, to show how his alleged recusancy enters into their significance and adds a new dimension unsuspected by those who cling to the conventional or naturalistic interpretation. It is in view of this added dimension that I would challenge all who reject the "recusant" interpretation as an unduly "sectarian" or "reductionist" restriction of Shakespeare's acknowledged universality. No, I answer, it is not this "recusant" interpretation of mine but their all too conventional, naturalistic interpretation that limits the universality of Shakespeare, by depriving it of this added dimension which alone accounts for the enigma of his genius and the intensity of his intonation especially in the tragedies. In their conventionalism, these scholars are paradoxically ready to patronize the widest diversity of eccentric interpretations for purposes of stage production, as well as the other strange interpretations that have arisen in recent years out of the theories of Marx, Freud and Derrida. Only, they are unwilling to admit this deeper dimension of a "recusant" interpretation, though it takes full account both of the plays themselves and of their historical background. They are even unwilling to accept it as a working hypothesis, which is all I ask of them from the outset. Such is the proverbial "narrowness of an open mind"!

Finally, I have to face the inevitable objection, made by all too many scholars today, that as everyone sees Shakespeare's plays in his own way, so Puritans will see them from a Puritan viewpoint, Anglicans from an Anglican viewpoint, and Catholics from a Catholic viewpoint – not to mention atheists and agnostics who see in the plays ample justification of their ways of thinking. And so, it is assumed, Jesuits like myself will see Shakespeare not just as a Catholic recusant but even as a secret sympathizer with the Jesuits, working hand in glove with them, if not precisely a Jesuit in disguise. Certainly, I wouldn't go so far as to maintain (according to the title of a book published in Chicago towards the beginning of this century) that "the Jesuits wrote Shakespeare", or that (as a Jesuit friend of mine has suggested) Shakespeare must have been a Jesuit novice during his "hidden" years. But I do maintain that there is ample evidence, far more than I have been able to present in this appendix, for a close connection between Shakespeare and English Jesuits from the time of his boyhood onwards, even before the time Campion passed through the county of Warwickshire in 1580 to the Northern county of Lancashire.

Anyhow, it is not so much a matter of who I am, whether a Catholic or not, whether a Jesuit or not, as of what I am saying and the evidence I am producing to justify what I say. All Shakespeare scholars, whether Catholic or not, or whether anti-Catholic or not, are subject to the same human limitations; and so we can't help seeing Shakespeare's plays with our own eyes and from our own points of view. Only, whereas most Shakespeare scholars are familiar enough with one side of the question, namely the text of the plays, all too few of them are familiar with the other side, namely the religious and specifically recusant background of the plays. Now it is in the light of this background that I have ventured to present my hypothesis of a hidden dimension of "recusant" meaning in the plays. So far from restricting or reducing the full richness of meaning in them, this interpretation I propose both accepts all that belongs to the level of a realistic or naturalistic reading and adds a dimension that throws new light on almost everything. It thus fulfils the conditions for a scientific hypothesis, that it should not just fit the known facts but rather fit them better than any other hypothesis; and this is my claim. At the same time, I would add, it is much more than a mere scientific hypothesis, such as remains on the pedestrian level of "knowledge": it is rather a precious key, even the only key, to unlock the hidden heart of Shakespeare and to sound the hitherto unsounded depths of his mystery – that which Shakespeare himself calls, in *Richard II*, "a strange brooch in this all-hating world", namely the brooch of love (v.5).

Bibliography

During the past century quite a number of books and articles have been published on Shakespeare and Catholicism in its various aspects. The first was by Henry Sebastian Bowden, a priest of the Oratory, entitled *The Religion of Shakespeare* (1899). He was no Shakespeare scholar, but he drew upon the papers left by the Victorian Shakespeare scholar, Richard Simpson, himself a friend and colleague of the great Cardinal Newman. Newman himself both in his letters and in a lecture on "Literature" included in his *Idea of a University* (1873), had previously stated his conviction that Shakespeare was at heart a Catholic.

The work begun by Bowden was carried on by the Jesuit scholar, Herbert Thurston, with special attention to Shakespeare's family and "the spiritual testament" of his father John Shakespeare, in two articles, "The Spiritual Testament of John Shakespeare" (*The Month* 1911) and "A Controverted Shakespeare Document" (*Dublin Review* 1923). His researches were further developed at book length by John Henry de Groot in *The Shakespeares and the Old Faith* (1946), including a special chapter on "Catholicism in the writings of William Shakespeare". A fuller biographical survey of *Shakespeare and Catholicism* (1952) was undertaken by two German scholars, Heinrich Mutschmann and Karl Wentersdorf; and their findings were summarized by M.D. Parker in a special Appendix, "Was Shakespeare a Recusant?", to her book, *The Slave of Life: A Study of Shakespeare and the Idea of Justice* (1955). A further useful summary of "Shakespeare's Faith" appears in the opening chapter of the Jesuit Christopher Devlin's *Hamlet's Divinity* (1963); and he also discusses Shakespeare's connection with the contemporary Jesuit martyr-poet Robert Southwell in his *Life of Robert Southwell* (1956).

All this material is used in biographies of Shakespeare by a number of Catholic authors, beginning with Clara Longworth, Comtesse de Chambrun, who brought out a series of books incorporating various revisions of her main thesis: *Shakespeare Actor-Poet* (1927), *Shakespeare Rediscovered* (1938) and *Shakespeare: A Portrait Restored* (1957). It was on the first of these books that G.K. Chesterton wrote a review article, published in his *Generally Speaking* (1928) and republished in my edition of his *Essays on Shakespeare* (1968). Less scholarly but more readable is Hugh Ross Williamson's book, *The Day Shakespeare Died* (1962), looking back over the life of Shakespeare in the light of the old tradition that "he died a papist". A further Catholic biography of Shakespeare is from the pen of the actor-scholar, Robert Speaight, *Shakespeare: The Man and His Achievement* (1977). Finally, in more recent years there is Ian Wilson's lengthy and detailed survey of *Shakespeare: The Evidence* (1993).

I might add my own study of *Shakespeare's Religious Background* (1973), in which I turn from the biographical to the more literary viewpoint, in an attempt to show how deeply Shakespeare's Catholicism entered into the deeper meaning of his plays. The same approach appears in my more recent *The Mediaeval Dimension of Shakespeare's Plays* (1990) and above all in the present volume.

About the Author

Peter Milward was born in London in 1925, studied at Wimbledon College 1933-43, entered the Society of Jesus 1943, studied philosophy at Heythrop College, Oxon. 1947-50, classical and English literature at Campion Hall, Oxford, 1950-54, came to Japan in 1954, studied Japanese, then theology at St. Mary's college, Tokyo (faculty of theology, Sophia University), 1571-61, was ordained priest 1960, began teacing in the department of English Literature, Sophia University, 1962. Specializing in Shakespearian drama, he published his first book, *An Introduction to Shakespeare's Plays*, 1964, followed by *Christian Themes in English Literature*, 1967. After further research at the Shakespeare Institute, Birmingham, 1965-66, he published *Shakespeare's Religious Background*, 1973; and as a result of subsequent research at the Huntington Library, Calfornia, he went on to publish two volumes of *Religious Contoversies of the Elizabethan Age* and *the Jacobean Age* in 1977 and 1978. Besides being vice-chairman of the Renaissance Institute of Sophia University, he is editor of "Renaissance Monographs" and of the Japanese *Renaissance Sōsho*; and with the opening of the Renaissance Centre in the new library of Sophia University in 1984, he was appointed its first director. He has also published books on G.M. Hopkins and T.S. Eliot, as well as many volumes of essays for Japanese students.